Also by

Joseph W. Michels

OUTBOUND FROM VIRGINIA [An historical novel]

BICYCLE DREAMS [An historical novel]

DECK PASSAGE [A memoir]

CHURCH [A William Church novel]

THE KINGSTONE RANSOM [A William Church novel]

FRENCH DIAMONDS [A William Church novel]

VILLA MARCKWALD [A romance novel]

POSTSTRASSE 16 [A thriller]

GABY [A biographical memoir]

ASSYRIAN GOLD [A William Church novel]

KAMINALJUYU CHIEFDOM: ABRIDGED [Archaeology]

CARR'S PT. [A thriller]

AKSUM

A REGIONAL PERSPECTIVE

Joseph W. Michels

AKSUM
A REGIONAL PERSPECTIVE

Copyright © 2017 Joseph W. Michels.

All rights reserved. No part of this book may be used or reproduced by any means, graphic, electronic, or mechanical, including photocopying, recording, taping or by any information storage retrieval system without the written permission of the author except in the case of brief quotations embodied in critical articles and reviews.

Original (unabridged) version entitled 'Changing Settlement Patterns in the Aksum-Yeha Region of Ethiopia: 700 BC - AD 850' published in 2005 by British Archaeological Reports, Oxford, UK.
Copyright © 2005 Joseph W. Michels.

Credit for cover art photo:
Copyright © Hecke61/Shutterstock.com

iUniverse books may be ordered through booksellers or by contacting:

iUniverse
1663 Liberty Drive
Bloomington, IN 47403
www.iuniverse.com
1-800-Authors (1-800-288-4677)

Because of the dynamic nature of the Internet, any web addresses or links contained in this book may have changed since publication and may no longer be valid. The views expressed in this work are solely those of the author and do not necessarily reflect the views of the publisher, and the publisher hereby disclaims any responsibility for them.

Any people depicted in stock imagery provided by Thinkstock are models, and such images are being used for illustrative purposes only.
Certain stock imagery © Thinkstock.

ISBN: 978-1-5320-2211-1 (sc)
ISBN: 978-1-5320-2212-8 (e)

Print information available on the last page.

iUniverse rev. date: 05/08/2017

TABLE OF CONTENTS

Preface ix

Introduction xi

Chapter One

    The Early Pre-Aksumite Period: Indigenous Rural Village Tradition versus the Yeha Enclave with its South Arabian Cultural Affinities 1

Chapter Two

    The Middle Pre-Aksumite Period: Ethio-Sabaean Hegemony, Irrigation Farming, and the Growth of Nucleated Communities 33

Chapter Three

    The Late Pre-Aksumite Period: The Eclipse of the Yeha Enclave Elite and the Rise of the Aksumite Chiefdom, and other Local Chiefdoms 47

Chapter Four

    The Early Aksumite Period: The Proliferation of Local Chiefdoms and the Emergence of the Aksumite Kingdom 73

Chapter Five
> The Late Aksumite Period: The Emergence of
> the State with Metropolitan Aksum as its Capital 102

Chapter Six
> The Early Post-Aksumite Period: The Collapse
> of the Aksumite Kingdom 133

Chapter Seven
> The Late Post-Aksumite Period: Population
> Collapse, Settlement Concealment, and the Rise
> of the Church as a Local Political Institution 142

Bibliographic Resources Used in the Preparation of the
Unabridged Publication 149

LIST OF FIGURES

Figure 1—Aksumite Archaeological Zone in NE Africa 88

Figure 2—Segment of Shirè Plateau in which the Archaeological Survey was conducted 89

Figure 3—Mai Agazen Basin, Early Pre-Aksumite Period.... 90

Figure 4—The Valley of Yeha: Early Pre-Aksumite Period....91

Figure 5—Subregional Settlement Groups, Early Pre-Aksumite Period 92

Figure 6—Middle Pre-Aksumite Settlement and Principal Sub-Regional Boundaries 93

Figure 7—Late Pre-Aksumite Settlement: Subregional Interaction Spheres... 94

Figure 8—Late Pre-Aksumite Settlement: Regional Political Organization... 95

Figure 9—Early Aksumite Elite Residential Structures........ 96

Figure 10—Early Aksumite Period: Early Phase Proliferation of Local Chiefdoms... 97

Figure 11—Early Aksumite Period: Late Phase Establishment of the Aksumite Capital............................... 98

Figure 12—Late Aksumite Settlement: Metropolitan Aksum and Peripheral Local Chiefdoms 99

Figure 13—Early Post-Aksumite Settlement: Regional Political Organization... 100

Figure 14—Late Post-Aksumite Settlement: Regional Political Organization...101

PREFACE

This work is an abridged version of the book CHANGING SETTLEMENT PATTERNS IN THE AKSUM-YEHA REGION OF ETHIOPIA: 700 BC—AD 850 written by the author and published in 2005 in the Cambridge Monographs in African Archaeology Series by British Archaeological Reports (BAR) of Oxford, UK.

By focusing on the interpreted findings in the original version it is hoped the fascinating story of the rise and fall of one of Africa's most remarkable civilizations, glimpsed through the prism of the settlement history of its most famous region, will become more accessible and more compelling. Towards this end, the work omits most of the original book's methodological and technical narrative, together with its many detailed site summaries.

This work is intended to serve a wider audience—those students, scholars and others who share a general interest in how emergent complex societies organize themselves as they undergo economic, demographic, religious and other societal changes.

The study of the archaeological traces of the Aksumite Civilization has a long and distinguished history beginning with the highly celebrated Deutsche Aksum Expedition (D.A.E.) of

1906 and continuing into the present. However, the principal archaeological evidence supporting the views expressed in this work comes from a 1974 archaeological survey of the region in question led by the author.

INTRODUCTION

The Aksum-Yeha Regional Survey was undertaken with the express purpose of providing an archaeological perspective on changing regional political organization in that portion of northern Ethiopia and Eritrea affected by the rise of the Aksumite kingdom (see Figure 1). The area in question extends from south of Makalé, the capital of the Ethiopian state of Tigray, to as far north as Asmara, the capital of Eritrea, and beyond.

Within that area, the French archaeologist, Francis Anfray, has mapped the distribution of over three-dozen important Aksumite or Pre-Aksumite sites (Anfray 1973a). Such sites generally exhibit the remains of monumental masonry architecture, and can best be regarded as principal centers—political, economic, and religious—of ancient local populations. How these centers and others yet to be discovered relate to a sustaining local population, and how they interrelate to form sub-regional, regional, and inter-regional networks are some of the basic questions that this survey addressed.

Within the Aksumite archaeological zone of northeast Africa, one region stood out as particularly important: the region extending from just west of the site of Aksum to just east of the site of Yeha (see Figure 2). It contained the principal political capitals of both the Pre-Aksumite era [Yeha] and of the Aksumite era [Aksum]. It has also benefitted from extensive archaeological examination—the site of Aksum alone has witnessed well over a dozen seasons of excavation. And much of the historical, numismatic, paleographic, and architectural research undertaken on that civilization has focused upon archaeological sites within that region. In short, what we believe we know about the Aksumite kingdom has for some time been largely a function of scholarly attention to the key events, personalities, local history, and archaeology of that region. It seemed, therefore, most appropriate to conduct a regional archaeological survey in that area, and to anticipate that the findings of the survey would be particularly relevant to contemporary and future efforts at historical and archaeological reconstruction of the Aksumite realm.

The Aksum-Yeha region is a segment of the Shiré plateau—a western extension of the Tigrean plateau. The land surface is a rolling upland 1900-2600 meters in elevation, rising steeply from the rugged valley systems of the Mareb and Tekezze rivers that lie to the north and south respectively.

The area has a dry, and at times very dry, period of ten months centered over the end of the calendar year (September to June). Annual rainfall ranges from 60 to 80 cm. The single rainfall season has a sharp maximum during July and August. Both are humid months and together receive 69% of the annual rainfall. It is colder during the rains of the summer than during the dry winter, with the monthly mean maximum temperature decreasing from 23 C in January to about 18 C during July and August, the wettest months.

At the present time, the region is grassland with scattered thorny brush and small trees, found especially on uncultivated hill slopes near streams and on the edges of cultivated fields. Extensive woods and forests are absent. However, Butzer (1981: 476) suggests *"that the "natural" plant cover was an open, mainly deciduous woodland.... with evergreen elements such as cedars, figs, and palms"*. This original plant cover, Butzer observes, would have obtained prior to agricultural settlement of the Shiré plateau and the subsequent degradation of the environment that such settlement presumably brought about.

During the survey a total of 201 square kilometers were systematically examined, representing a 28% sample of the survey region. Given the application of a stratified random sampling model, there is every expectation that the 28% of the survey region examined is representative of the region as a whole, and that one can usefully extrapolate from the archaeological record uncovered in the sample to the survey region in its entirety. The likelihood of this being the case is further strengthened by the fact that in the case of half of the 5x5 sq. km grid units sampled, particularly those that comprised the most favorable settings for habitation, the actual percentage of land examined exceeded 40%. The most glaring instances of under-sampling occurred in the vicinity of the town of Adua.

That locale was scheduled for survey towards the end of the field season, but could not be adequately covered due to the political unrest in that area associated with the events that ultimately resulted the overthrow of Emperor Haile Sellassie.

CHAPTER ONE
The Early Pre-Aksumite Period

THE NATURE OF SOUTH ARABIAN CONTACT

Evidence suggests that rural farming hamlets and villages probably date back to 1500 BC, but chronological controls used in this study make it likely that continuous, widespread settlement of the survey region by farmer/pastoralists begins during the latter part of the 8th Century or by the first half of the 7th Century BC. Sometime during that era or shortly afterwards a South Arabian cultural presence can be detected. Of continuing interest to Aksumite researchers is what brought about the introduction of South Arabian cultural traits into the northern highlands of Ethiopia.

Several scenarios logically present themselves. First, the indigenous population could have periodically hosted short-term trading expeditions from across the Red Sea, receiving in exchange for local commodities trade wares and other manufactured goods originating in South Arabia or from elsewhere within the far flung camel caravan network. A second scenario might be one involving the actual colonization of selected areas of the highlands by whole communities of South

Arabians. A third scenario might involve the establishment of mercantile elites within the Ethiopian highlands who were few in number but who displayed facets of South Arabian culture that contributed to their high prestige.

The archaeological correlates of these scenarios can be provisionally defined. In the case of the first scenario one would perhaps expect to find trade wares and other exotic artifacts to occur in local communities. One would however probably not expect to find fully functioning South Arabian institutions grafted onto the landscape. In the second scenario one would probably expect to observe contrasting settlement patterns that correlated with contrasting material cultures. In the third scenario it would be precisely the opposite. Foreign artifacts would be concentrated in and around the residences and institutional enclaves of this South Arabian elite while leaving the material culture of the local communities largely unaffected.

The archaeological record of the Early Pre-Aksumite Period—the time during which South Arabian cultural traits first appear in the Ethiopian highlands—offers several lines of evidence with which to evaluate these competing hypotheses: (1) imported institutional artifacts and architecture; (2) community types and settlement pattern; (3) ceramic analysis.

South Arabian cultural traits appear to be concentrated at four sites within the survey area during this period: the Yeha Temple, Grat Beal Gubri, Abba Pentaleon, and Enda Cerqos. In each case, one observes the remains of dressed-stone masonry architecture believed to represent the remains of religious structures of monumental aspect. Both the masonry technique employed, as well as their architectural style, point to South Arabian origins. Objects of a special religious nature such as stelae and stone altars were found in the immediate vicinity of the Yeha Temple complex, and masonry elements with Sabaean inscriptions are associated with the Yeha Temple, Abba Pentaleon, and Enda Cerqos.

Analysis of community types and settlement pattern show that among the 35 residential communities identified in the survey that date to this period there appears to be a rather dramatic contrast in settlement pattern. On that portion of the Shirè Plateau that is in the vicinity of Aksum a settlement system dominated by *hamlets* and *small villages* is to be found. In contrast, there appears to be a deficit of settlements in the Adua basin and in the rugged Adua-Yeha corridor while at the same time a large population is concentrated at a single site in the valley of Yeha. The settlement system in the valley of Yeha, with its complex of monumental religious structures grouped on high ground overlooking the fertile, irrigated fields of the valley floor and in clear view of the large town located on terraces on the opposite side of the valley, is highly reminiscent of the plan of the Sabaean capital of Marib in South Arabia.

Ceramic analysis, involving *ware* taxonomy, decorative treatment and vessel lip morphology, has contributed to our ability to construct a more dynamic picture of the interaction of communities on a regional scale. Among the findings were several that touch directly upon the question of the nature of South Arabian contact. First, there is no evidence of an exotic complex of ceramic types associated with any community in the survey area. Second, although the survey area appears to contain at least three ceramically definable local populations all seem to reflect indigenous ceramic traditions.

When we combine the several lines of evidence summarized above, it becomes possible to evaluate alternative scenarios of South Arabian cultural contact. The first scenario, that the indigenous population hosted short-term trading expeditions from across the Red Sea is not supported. The archaeological correlates are simply not present: trade wares and other exotic artifacts do not occur generally among local communities, while in fact there is evidence of the presence of South Arabian cultural institutions (i.e. religious) prominent on the landscape.

The second scenario, involving an actual colonization of selected areas of the Ethiopian highlands by whole communities of South Arabians, is also not supported. For although there is evidence of contrasting settlement patterns as one would expect under this scenario, there is no accompanying contrast in material culture. Furthermore, the contrasting settlement patterns appear to be explainable by postulating a redeployment and residential nucleation of some portion of an existing, indigenous population rather than the insertion of an immigrant population.

The final scenario, that mercantile elites displaying South Arabian cultural traits established themselves at key points in the Ethiopian Highlands, is strongly supported by the concentration of imported institutional architecture and artifacts and by the prominence given to such institutional features, presumably to enhance prestige. Further support is given by the fact that the material culture of residential communities throughout the survey area was unaffected.

One can conclude that South Arabian cultural affinities associated with the Early Pre-Aksumite Period were introduced by a small number of elite families who appear to have taken up residence in the Vally of Yeha for the purpose of coordinating the procurement and transport of African commodities in support of South Arabian caravan networks.

The conspicuous monumental architecture associated with South Arabian religious institutions seems to far exceed a scale commensurate with the needs of a small residential elite, however. One can speculate that the grand scale of the institutional precincts was designed to enhance the prestige of the elite in the eyes of the indigenous population and thus to draw them into the socio-economic orbit of the newly established enclave.

The success of this quest can perhaps be seen in the apparent concentration of the local population of the Adua-Yeha Corridor, the Yeha Valley, and perhaps the Adua Basin, in the *large town* of Enda Gully. The resulting settlement plan mirrored that of

Marib and by analogy it would be reasonable to suppose that a comparable focus on irrigation agriculture was also present. Whether the technology of stream-fed irrigation systems was introduced from South Arabia at this time or was already a local option is not an answerable question. What does seem clear, however, is that the large scale of such systems that is implied by the concentration of population in the Valley of Yeha during this period, and by comparable population redeployments in the vicinity of Aksum during the subsequent period, was related to successful efforts at the socio-economic integration and control of some fraction of the local population, particularly communities within subregions in and around the Valley of Yeha.

THE *KINGDOM OF DA'AMAT*

Inscriptions recovered from various sites that exhibit South Arabian cultural features allude to the existence of a *Kingdom of Da'amat*. Scholars have argued that such a polity should be interpreted as an indigenous one, but one that has strong links with South Arabia—most likely as a result of trade networks that bound the two areas together. The term *'ethio-sabaean'* has sometimes been used to describe the polity out of consideration for the profound assimilation of South Arabian cultural traits by the leadership of this indigenous entity that is apparently reflected in the archaeology of key sites with which the polity is associated.

On epigraphic and archaeological grounds, the *Kingdom of Da'amat* is believed to have appeared at the outset of the Early Pre-Aksumite Period, and to have flourished throughout that period. Sites with large South Arabian temples, such as Yeha are believed to have served as principal centers of the kingdom; suggesting that the kingdom was of inter-regional scope.

DiBlasi has argued (2004a) that the apparent sudden appearance of South Arabian monumental architecture, writing, religious ideology and symbolism in Eritrea/Ethiopia is strong evidence for there having been a small group of South Arabian settlers who were responsible for the initial establishment of their culture in the Horn of Africa. This pioneering group, probably including skilled craftsmen (architects, builders, stonemasons, and artists) as well as a cadre of religious personnel created centers, such as Yeha, which attracted nearby indigenous populations. DiBlasi argues, further, that such centers served to stimulate an acculturative process that led to the assimilation and eventual transformation of South Arabian culture by the indigenous population. Over time, according to DiBlasi, local populations were increasingly drawn into *Da'amat* society, but in the process they transformed the *Da'amat* polity into one that can most accurately be described as *ethio-sabaean*.

The archeological picture presented in this chapter is fully compatible with the general thesis regarding the *Kingdom of Da'amat* put forward by Fattovich and others, as well as with the acculturative scenario argued by DiBlasi.

Joseph W. Michels

ECOLOGICAL OBSERVATIONS

Ecozones are defined in terms of soil characteristics. They reflect the way contemporary farmers view the land as reported during ethnographic survey, together with the kind of parent rock material with which each is associated. Seven ecozones have been defined. But in addition to folk taxonomies of soil and their underlying geology, it is also useful to factor in characteristic landforms. The survey region consists of three principal landforms: (1) lands consisting of deeply cut alluvial features, (2) low gradient arable lands, and (3) lands with strong vertical relief.

Ethnobotanical notes obtained during ethnographic survey make it clear that there is a basic set of cultigens that can be farmed in any ecozone and on any land form. They include wheat, barley, tef, finger millet, and beans. Sorghum and maize tend to be confined to Ecozones I and II, but in association with all three landforms. And Endate, a local grain, tends to be confined to Ecozones IV and V; particularly on lands with strong vertical relief. Also associated with landforms of strong vertical relief is the cultivation of such specialty items as nug (oil seed) and flax.

What these findings suggest is that the principal ecological variables affecting community placement would seem to be practical ones such as fallowing cycles, potential for irrigation, ease of plow cultivation, grazing potential for livestock, and proximity to a domestic water supply.

A total of 35 residential communities and four special structures were encountered during survey that date to the Early Pre-Aksumite period. Among the 35 sites recorded, 12 are located in areas associated with deep alluvial features where the potential for irrigation and livestock grazing, and proximity to a domestic water supply is evident. Eighteen sites are located on or near low-gradient arable lands, where plow cultivation can be practiced with ease. Only four sites are located in areas that have strong vertical relief, and these are all hamlet-sized settlements.

When one considers site distribution with respect to soil-defined ecozones, the apparent diversity of site placement choices with respect to ecological variables is further reinforced. One-third of the sites were located on premium soils (Ecozones I and II). One-third were located on soils that require a fallowing cycle or fertilization but which are amenable to irrigation, given the prevailing landform. While the remaining one-third were located on soils that require some form of fertility intervention and yet are not amenable to irrigation.

It is only when we focus on site variablility with respect to estimated population that the underlying ecological priorities begin to emerge. A full 75% of the population estimated on the basis of the 35 sites recorded occupied lands that are characterized by premium soils (Ecozones I and II). These are soils that require little if any fertility intervention while supporting annual cropping. Only a minority of 25% of the population occupied one of the other ecozones where fallowing cycles or fertilization or both complicate the farming endeavor. A second ecological priority is access to deeply cut alluvial features, such as valleys or gorges. While only 13 of 35 sites are located on or adjacent to such landforms, they account for 72% of the estimated population. Only 8% of the estimated population are to be found in areas that do not reflect one or the other of the two ecological priorities: premium soils or alluvial bottomlands.

IRRIGATION FARMING

It has often been assumed that irrigation farming was introduced into the Ethiopian Highlands by South Arabian immigrants. But the indigenous settlement pattern as reflected in the Early Pre-Aksumite Period would suggest that small-scale, stream-fed systems may have much earlier origins. Simoons (1960:74) observes that in the highlands irrigated plots are *small and inconspicuous*, and occur only in areas where the water from streams can be easily diverted to adjacent fields by means of shallow ditches. He reports that farmers prepare such systems in order to make cultivation possible during the dry season. Both his survey and that of the present author confirm the impression that traditional farmers rely principally on rainfall to water their crops, and seem prepared to endure the risk of crop loss through drought rather than invest the labor to construct elaborate irrigation works.

It is the distinction between small-scale, rudimentary irrigation systems and a more labor-intensive, large-scale option that is useful in analyzing the impact of South Arabia on indigenous farming strategies of the Ethiopian plateau. In the Early Pre-Aksumite Period, both strategies appear to be represented.

THE MAI AGAZEN BASIN: A CASE STUDY IN INDIGENOUS IRRIGATION

The Mai Agazen Basin is a narrow, alluvial depression located at the extreme southern edge of the Plain of Aksum (see Figure 3). It is one of a number of such southern escarpment drainage features. All tend to be relatively narrow and deeply cut. The volume of stream flow varies with the season. But even under conditions of drought (as in 1974), when stream flow was interrupted, water tables remain high, supporting luxuriant grassy pasture for livestock, and even pools of standing water.

The Mai Agazen Basin has a north-south orientation and extends for about two and one-half kilometers. It ranges from 200 to 400 meters in width, constrained by steep-sided escarpments parallel to one another on the east and west that rise up to form tablelands or mesas. The maximum land surface in the basin on which irrigated crops could be cultivated is hard to estimate accurately. If only rudimentary irrigation works were established, up to 15 hectares could possibly be farmed. This assumes that the plots comprise a one and one-half kilometer long strip, 100 meters wide, centered on the stream itself. With impoundment levees, longer feed canals, and some terracing it would probably have been possible to irrigate as much as 40 hectares of land within the basin.

The parent rock of the Mai Agazen Basin consists of limestone and dolomite. The local soil is a brown sandy loam, identified by resident farmers as Chincha Ba`akel [B] (Ecozone V). One kilometer north of the basin is the southern edge of the Plain of Aksum with its rich, black clay soil known locally as Welka [A] (Ecozone I).

Despite the proximity of the region's finest soils (Welka), in an area that is only very lightly settled, three Early Pre-Aksumite communities chose to locate themselves within 500 meters of each other on opposing bluffs overlooking the Mai Agazen Basin. These are Melazo (55-51-098), Adi Berekti (65-11-004, and Adi Berekti (65-11-031). Melazo is believed to have been a small village of just under 200 persons. The two Adi Berekti sites are believed to have been hamlets of 35 and 12 people respectively.

The tight cluster of sites, their placement on the immediate summits of the two opposing escarpments that form the basin, the fact that superior soils for dry farming (with comparable access to drinking water) were available only one kilometer away, make a compelling argument for the hypothesis that stream-fed irrigation was a primary focus around which settlement decisions were made by this set of communities. But given the modest size of the total estimated population for the three communities along the Mai Agazen Basin, it seems reasonable to suppose that such a focus involved only small-scale irrigation works like those described by Simoons.

THE VALLEY OF YEHA: A CASE STUDY IN SOUTH ARABIAN IRRIGATION

Urban communities in South Arabia all featured sophisticated irrigation systems. The systems were not designed to tap perennial rivers or to impound large quantities of seasonal runoff, but rather to quickly harness rain-fed streams by means of an elaborate system of canals and channels. To maximize the total field area served by the irrigation system, dams were sometimes built across the beds of principal streams to impound sufficient water so that sluice gates at either end of the dam could discharge water at a high enough elevation that gravity feed would disperse the waters even into fields at the upper margins of the valley floor.

The largest and most famous dam was the one located at Marib, the capital of the Kingdom of Saba. Portions of it are still in evidence. The dam was built of earth with a dressed stone facing. Sluice gates at either end fed canals and a network of channels that distributed the waters over an area estimated at around 1600 hectares (Van Beek 1969:43).

The key features of South Arabian irrigation that seems to set it off from possibly indigenous, small-scale systems such as that hypothesized for the Mai Agazen Basin are (a) maximization of irrigated area, and (b) large-scale earthen and masonry structures to accomplish the former. The archaeological record of the Valley of Yeha for the Early Pre-Aksumite Period has not yet revealed evidence of the latter, but topography, hydrology, and settlement pattern point compellingly to the former.

The Valley of Yeha consists of a series of interconnected basins (see Figure 4) surrounded by rugged hills. Fed by the hillside watershed, a network of streams passes through the basins and drain towards the northeast. Aerial photographs taken in the early 1960's reveal a widely dispersed high water table comprising approximately one half of the aggregate basin floor. And even during the extremely dry conditions observed in the spring of 1974 some portions of the basins were being utilized agriculturally, either as irrigated fields or grazing lands for sizable livestock herds.

The basins of the Valley of Yeha reveal a patchwork of rectangular field plots, many of which even in 1974 were linked by a network of earthen ditches to the nearest principal stream. Deep erosional gulleys that might otherwise impede gravity flow of water were bridged with hollow logs in those areas where the fields were under active cultivation. Nowhere else in the survey region did we observe such extensive traces of stream-fed, ditch irrigation. It is estimated that the combined set of interconnected basins that form the Valley of Yeha could have provided as much as 185 hectares of irrigated farmland.

Apparently capitalizing upon the uniquely advantageous ecological characteristics of the Valley of Yeha—fertile Welka soils and the potential for large-scale irrigation farming—mercantile elites with strong South Arabian cultural ties established a center. Archaeological evidence of South Arabian cultural traits in the survey region dating to this period is primarily located here. The only exceptions so far documented are the structure at Abba Pentaleon (near Aksum), and the residue of the structure at Enda Cerqos (in the Mai Agazen Basin).

Maximization of irrigation in the Valley of Yeha during this period was made likely if for no other reason than that the large, nucleated population of the valley might have required it. The site of Enda Gully—located on a hill situated between the two principal basins of the valley—is believed to represent the remains of a large town occupied by approximately 3500 people. In addition, adjacent to the Yeha Temple are the remains of a small village of about 250 people (Grat Abune Afsea). Together, these communities constitute 55% of the total population of the survey region as estimated from directly observable site remains despite the fact that the Valley of Yeha represents only about two percent of the 201 square kilometers actually surveyed!

Several key features of the community plan of South Arabian *Marib* appear to have been replicated at Yeha. First, the town of Marib was physically separate from the town's principal temple: the *Haram Bilkis*. This was also true for Yeha: the town—Enda

Joseph W. Michels

Gully—is spatially separate from the cluster of temple and religious structures consisting of the Yeha Temple and Grat Belai Gubri. Second, the distance between the town and the temple precinct at Marib was one kilometer. That is the exact distance separating Enda Gully from the Yeha temple precinct. Third, the town/temple axis cuts perpendicularly through the long axis of the central basin under irrigation. In the case of Marib the axis cuts across the basin of the Wadi Dhana (below the dam). In the case of Yeha the axis cuts across the widest and most central of the interconnected basins.

And finally, the town/temple precinct axis was surrounded by irrigated fields. In the case of Marib the town was within the field system supplied by the northern sluice gate of the dam, while the Haram Bilkis was within the field system supplied by southern sluice gate. In Yeha, the town of Enda Gully was on a hill surrounded on three sides by potentially irrigable lands, while the Yeha Temple precinct was on a small hill also surrounded on three sides by potentially irrigable lands.

The compelling similarity in community planning, the concentration of South Arabian architecture and artifacts, the extraordinary nucleation of population, and the unique potential for maximizing irrigation potential all suggest that the Valley of Yeha represents the best example currently available of what was involved in the implementation of South Arabian settlement and agricultural strategy during the Early Pre-Aksumite Period.

COMMUNITY PATTERNING

Four different community types have been observed among the archaeological remains of the Early Pre-Aksumite Period. They include *hamlets*, *small* and *large villages*, and a *large town*. Thirty of the 35 communities dating to this period were either *hamlets* or *small villages*, yet they account for only 29% of the total population estimated directly from the recorded sites. Clearly, there was an underlying complexity to community patterning that requires discussion.

There are two aspects of community patterning to be addressed: the geographical distribution of communities by type, and the extent to which one can discern groupings of these communities that reflect the manner in which social and political factors have organized the regional population into spatially discrete local populations.

The Aksum-Yeha Survey Region can be divided into four principal physiographic areas, with constituent subdivisions. For the 201 sq. km. actually surveyed site density averaged 0.17 sites per sq. km., and estimated population for this period based on an analysis of actually recorded sites averaged 35 persons per sq. km. The following discussion points up just how widely each of the four physiographic zones diverged from such benchmark averages.

The Aksumite Plateau, with 38% of the area surveyed, revealed an average of 0.21 sites/sq. km. and an estimated population of 24 persons per sq. km. The area comes closest to matching the benchmark averages for the survey region as a whole. The plain and its constituent *amba* formations, together with the Southern Drainage Systems contained the largest number of discrete communities—primarily *hamlets* and *small villages*—spaced some two to four kilometers apart on average. Although there were four *large villages* in the plateau area they do not [as a class] appear to function as central places in any political or economic sense. Smaller communities are not clustered in satellite fashion around them, nor do they contain any special architectural features. However two of the four *large villages* are located near the South Arabian religious structures of Abba Pentaleon and Enda Cerqos respectively, suggesting the possibility that these two in particular might represent residential outliers of the Yeha Enclave, and of the *Da'amat Polity* that it presumably represents.

Despite the predominance of small communities, the Aksumite Plateau contained some 43% of the total estimated regional population based on actual sites discovered. About a third of the population resided in the southern drainage areas, probably capitalizing on opportunities to practice the kind of indigenous irrigation farming discussed earlier in connection with the Mai Agazen Basin. The other two-thirds are to be found in close proximity to the rich soils of Ecozones I & II out on the plain proper or on the *amba* formations that dot the plain. Here, dry farming would be an optimal strategy. The Western and Northern Peripheries of the Aksumite Plateau were only very lightly settled.

Surface survey of the Adua Basin Area was adversely affected by the political unrest associated with the ongoing revolution of 1974 that ultimately did away with the monarchical regime of Ethiopia. Free movement by the survey team in the Adua basin proper was problematic just as this area was scheduled for survey. As a result, only a small portion of the basin proper was examined and only one site dating to the Early Pre-Aksumite Period was detected. Our picture of community patterning in the Adua basin proper may thus be in error. Given the relatively high density of estimated population in the southern drainage systems of the Aksumite Plateau (45 persons/sq. km.) the Adua basin proper—equally amenable to small-scale irrigation systems—should have accommodated a comparably high density. Although the absence of close-by Welka soils (Ecozone I) may call into question the true comparability of the two areas.

With 17% of the 128 sq. km. of the Adua Basin Area surveyed, only two sites datable to the Early Pre-Aksumite Period were discovered: a *small village* and one *hamlet*. The resulting averages are 0.09 sites per sq. km. and an estimated population density of 6 persons per sq. km. A suggestion that these remarkably low figures might actually by accurate, however, is given by focusing on the Western Hills portion where a respectable 20% of the area was surveyed without political complications and still yielded only one site datable to this period. In addition, the Adua-Yeha Corridor Area survey produced comparably low indices despite an 18% sample survey under routine conditions.

The Adua-Yeha Corridor consists of sinuous valley systems and adjacent mountainous areas. The former serve as natural transit corridors connecting the Adua basin and the interconnecting basins of the Yeha area to the east. Ample opportunities to practice small-scale irrigation are provided throughout the rugged corridor, as contemporary farming patterns demonstrate. And even the steep slopes and high maintenance soils of the mountainous areas were amply populated during recent times. Despite this agricultural potential, a survey of 18% of the Corridor's 184 sq. km surface yielded only two sites datable to the Early Pre-Aksumite Period: one *small village* and one *hamlet*. Site density is thus even lower than in the Adua Basin Area—0.06 sites per sq. km.—and estimated population density is comparably low: 6 persons per sq. km.

Two alternative hypotheses offer an explanation for the remarkably low population densities detected in the Adua Basin and Adua-Yeha Corridor Areas. One is an ecological hypothesis that follows from the analysis given earlier in this chapter. Namely, that total population was sufficiently low in the survey region as a whole that communities had the luxury of limiting settlement to Ecozones I and II, or to alluvial features within other ecozones but where there was also close proximity to Ecozones I and II. As was pointed out earlier, this hypothesis can explain one aspect of community patterning for 92% of the Early Pre-Aksumite population.

The second hypothesis is a political one, namely, that those families that normally would have comprised the indigenous population of the Adua Basin and Adua-Yeha Corridor Areas are to be found among the peoples forming the large, nucleated population of the Yeha Valley. This is a political hypothesis in the sense that the carrying capacity of the Yeha Valley is believed to have been dramatically augmented by the introduction of large-scale, South Arabian-style irrigation systems.

The two hypotheses are not incompatible. Augmenting the carrying capacity of the Yeha Valley, which exhibits both key features of preferred settlement choices—premium soils and irrigation potential—meant that South Arabian intervention permitted a higher fraction of the indigenous population to be accommodated within the preferred ecological setting.

The paucity of settlements detected within the Adua Basin and the Adua-Yeha Corridor Areas and the extraordinary nucleation of the population in the Yeha Valley Area strongly suggests that the indigenous farming population of the survey region as a whole—albeit present as early as 1500 BC—experienced most of its initial growth <u>during</u> the years of South Arabian contact. For otherwise, one would detect numerous <u>abandoned</u> sites as the extant population was politically induced to nucleate within the Yeha Valley. Such a phenomenon is observable in the transition between the Early Pre-Aksumite

Period and the Middle Pre-Aksumite Period, thus its absence in the archaeological record documenting the transition to the Early Pre-Aksumite Period is noteworthy.

As can be surmised by the above comments, the Yeha Valley Area has a distinctive community pattern during the period under discussion. The area comprises 67 sq. km. with 28% of the area having been surveyed. Only four sites were detected that dated to the Early Pre-Aksumite Period, yielding an average site density of 0.21 sites per sq. km. – very close to the average site density for the survey region as a whole (0.17/sq. km.). Yet one of those sites, Enda Gully, had an estimated population of about 3500, producing an average population density of 196 persons per sq. km. This is six times the average population density for the survey region as a whole! Enda Gully was the only *town* settlement among the 35 sites documented for this phase. Its uniqueness and its association with an impressive cluster of South Arabian style buildings of monumental scale, in an ecological setting uniquely suited for large-scale irrigation farming, has already been discussed in an earlier section of this chapter.

In summary, community patterning within the survey region as a whole was not uniform during the Early Pre-Aksumite Period. Three patterns present themselves: (a) numerous small-scale settlements scattered widely over the landscape (the Aksumite Plateau model); (b) fugitive small-scale settlements located in essentially unpopulated areas (the Adua Basin & Adua-Yeha

Corridor model); (c) nucleation of a subregional population into a single *town*-sized settlement (the Yeha Valley model). What remains to be explored are the organizational features, to the extent that they are discernible archaeologically, that result in a coherent regional picture of sociopolitical structure.

SETTLEMENT SYSTEM

Ethnoarchaeological surveys conducted by project personnel revealed that the 1974 population of the Aksum-Yeha Survey Region was organized into six geographically definable subregions on the basis of the participation of community households in one or another of six market centers: Wukro, Aksum, Mehara Dagou, Adua, Yeha, and Faras Mai. Other potential organizing mechanisms that might promote the formation of discrete interaction spheres within the ethnographic present are (1) the church affiliation of rural communities, and (2) the attraction of governmental services (such as food distribution during droughts) located at municipal centers such as Aksum and Adua. However created, such subregions promote greater degrees of sharing of distinctive cultural traits as interaction among households within a given subregion is intensified, while interaction among households of differing subregions is reduced.

Ceramics is probably one of the most useful elements of material culture with which to analyze inter-community interaction. It's plasticity of form, decoration, manufacture, and choice of materials permits the emergence of a distinct ceramic micro-tradition among communities that participate in a given subregional interaction sphere. And the absence of such ceramic micro-traditions might indicate the absence of organizational constraints; indeed, it might indicate systematic political, social or economic integration of the communities in question.

For the purposes of this study, ceramics constitute the only archaeological evidence available, other than community patterning. It is fortunate that its potential as a basis for settlement system analysis is so favorable. Three categories of ceramic variables were independently analyzed for each archaeological phase: (1) ceramic ware, (2) vessel decorative treatment, and (3) vessel lip form.

CERAMIC WARE

A computer-assisted seriation of site assemblages with respect to ceramic ware was undertaken for the purpose of generating site chronological placement. Among the 35 sites dating to the Early Pre-Aksumite Period, 28 fell within a single computer-generated Cluster and six were located on the immediate periphery of that Cluster in the final seriational ordering. All 35 sites were ultimately assignable to a single cluster.

Since the analysis of relative ware frequencies among archaeological assemblages was the fundamental basis for defining the Early Pre-Aksumite Period and in determining site membership within that period, it is clear that all 35 sites must share a relatively uniform ceramic signature at that level of ceramic comparison. As a result, ware analysis was not employed in differentiating subregional aggregates of sites within the Early Pre-Aksumite Period.

It is on this level of comparison, however, that one can ask the question raised earlier in this chapter regarding the nature of the South Arabian presence. If all Early Pre-Aksumite sites in the region shared a common ceramic tradition with respect to ware preferences then no community or set of communities stands out as exhibiting an exotic ceramic tradition, which might have been the basis for postulating actual colonization of the region by South Arabia.

VESSEL DECORATIVE TREATMENT

All 786 sherds in Early Pre-Aksumite site assemblages for which decorative treatment was in evidence were coded. The coding protocol contained 91 variants that represent a wide variety of decorative technique/design permutations. Only 23 of the 91 variants were encountered among the Early Pre-Aksumite assemblages. And two—*grooved simple linear* (DT43), *grooved complex linear* (DT44)—comprised almost three-quarters of the coded sherds. Given their ubiquity throughout the survey region they had no discriminant function. Analysis thus rested upon the remaining 234 sherds and 21 attribute states.

Given the small number of specimens, an initial comparison of sites was carried out only with respect to decorative technique, eliminating consideration of decorative design variation. This reduced the number of taxonomic categories from 23 to 7. Nevertheless, since the number of sherds that exhibited discriminating attributes within any given site assemblage was so small it was not possible to conduct the kind of rigorous quantitative analysis that characterized the study of ceramic wares. Instead, a more straightforward arithmetic comparison was undertaken using actual counts and percentages.

Spatially contiguous sites were grouped together to form observational units. This was done with the expectation that it would reveal spatial clusters of sites exhibiting distinctive attribute features. Site groupings used in the study were designed to maximize potential contrasts, and in particular to further test the South Arabian colonization hypothesis. For example, the sites in the immediate vicinity of two of the South Arabian architectural complexes—Abba Pentaleon and the Yeha temple/Grat Beal Gubri complex—constituted two separate groupings under the assumption that they were the most likely candidates if indeed colonial communities were present. Similarly, the sites along the southern periphery of the Aksumite Plateau were grouped together since this was an area that exhibited South Arabian cultural affinities during the subsequent Middle Pre-Aksumite Period. Additional site groupings were defined in conformity with the geographic subdivisions defined earlier.

Using the mean and standard deviation values (expressed in percentages) as a benchmark, it is apparent that the Adua & Adua/Yeha Corridor site group contrasts with the Aksumite Plain/Northern Periphery group with respect to the relative frequency of *incised* and *grooved* decorative treatment. The latter group also exhibits some distinctiveness in the occurrence of *ribbed* and *fluted* sherds, albeit in modest frequencies. And the Yeha Valley group shows a similar distinctiveness in the percentage of *notched* sherds.

Taken alone, these differences allow one to draw only very modest inferences. They suggest (1) a possible subregional boundary between the Aksumite Plateau geographic zone and the adjacent geographic zones to the east: Adua and the Adua/Yeha Corridor. And (2) they make clear that the Yeha Valley group cannot be regarded as exotic even at this level of ceramic characterization, for despite the group's percentage of *notched* sherds, this type of decorative treatment actually occurs in trace frequencies at more sites on the western periphery of the Aksumite Plateau than anywhere else within the survey region during this period. The latter finding adds further evidence disconfirming the South Arabian colonization hypothesis.

VESSEL LIP FORM

All rim sherds collected were coded for lip form. The coding protocol contained 48 variants. Of those 48, six were too common in the Early Pre-Aksumite Period to serve as useful attributes. Twenty-one variants were either never encountered or occurred very rarely. The remaining 21 variants were potentially diagnostic.

The occurrence of each of the 21 potentially diagnostic variants was plotted on a regional map showing the spatial distribution of the 34 Early Pre-Aksumite sites. Eight of the lip form variants proved to be of some utility in defining (albeit provisionally) spatially discrete groupings of sites. The remaining 13 variants revealed no discernible distributional pattern.

The eight lip forms are LF-*bolstered, rounded*; LF-*wedge, bilateral*; LF-*wedge, bilateral, grooved*; LF-*wedge, internal*; LF-*thickened, externally, flat*; LF-*external bolster, large taper*; LF-*thickened, external taper*; LF-*thickened, internal taper*. When combined with decorative treatment variants DT-*notched fillet body* and DT-*ribbed* three geographic sub-regions come into focus.

Rim sherds exhibiting one or another of four lip forms—*wedge* variants or *bolstered*—appear to be diagnostic of Early Pre-Aksumite communities located in the central portion of the Aksumite Plateau. Some 64% of all sherds with these lip forms are to be found in that area. Communities in the southwest portion of the Aksumite Plateau, on the other hand, account for 25%, and communities in the Adua/Yeha area only account for 11%.

In contrast, some 63% of sherds with *notched fillet body* or *ribbed* decorative treatment, or with *thickened externally, flat* lip form are to be found in the southwest portion of the Aksumite Plateau, and can reasonably be considered diagnostic of that subregion. Similarly, the Adua/Yeha subregion is distinctive in that some 92% of sherds with *taper* variants of lip form are to be found there.

Figure 5 displays the resulting boundaries of the three subregions revealed by the distribution of diagnostic ceramic attribute clusters.

CONCLUSIONS

The survey region appears to contain at least three ceramically definable local populations during the Early Pre-Aksumite Period: (1) communities located on the Plain of Aksum, the central *amba* formations, and most of the Southern Drainage Systems, collectively referred to as *Aksum-Central*; (2) communities in the hills of the Western Periphery of the Aksumite Plateau together with the extreme western *amba* formations and Southern Drainage Systems, referred to as *Aksum-Southwest*; and (3) communities in the Adua Basin, the Adua-Yeha Corridor, and the Yeha Valley System, collectively referred to as *Adua/Yeha* (see Figure 5).

Sites associated with South Arabian architecture and artifacts were not diffentiated from sites without such associations in the spatial solution arrived at through ceramic analysis. Two of the three subregions hosted South Arabian cultural features but posed sharp contrasts in their respective diagnostic ceramic attributes (i.e. *Aksum-Central* and *Adua/Yeha*).

One must infer that whatever personnel were associated with the South Arabian cultural manifestations of this period they constituted an elite cadre insufficient in number to have had any noticeable effect on ceramic assemblage formation at communities with which they must have been associated. There is no support within the provisional ceramic analysis undertaken to assert that any of the communities within the survey region were comprised principally of colonists from South Arabia or anywhere else outside the Aksumite *culture area*.

Nevertheless, the two principal Yeha communities—Enda Gully and Grat Abune Afsea—are distinguished from all others by the diversity of their ceramic assemblages and by the presence of ceramic attribute variants associated with local populations located elsewhere in the survey region. The Yeha communities appeared to have enjoyed special access to pottery vessels that were stylistically associated with other local populations within the region. This suggests that Yeha was a regional center visited by diverse local populations. Given the imposing temple architecture at Yeha, it seems reasonable to conjecture that these visits were connected to religious activities or to market activities associated with religious activities.

Thus Yeha does not appear to have been a South Arabian colonial enclave set apart from the indigenous population but a fully integrated demographic, cultural, economic, and ritual center.

The remarkable concentration of population within the town of Enda Gully demonstrates the attraction South Arabian cultural features had on the local population. Carrying capacity of local agriculture must have been substantially augmented by the maximization of irrigation within the Yeha basin sponsored by an elite responsible for introducing South Arabian cultural elements into the area. And the large resident population would have stimulated commerce and very likely resulted in Yeha becoming a *market town* of regional importance. Contributing to the commercial prominence of Yeha would have been its status as a procurement center for exportable commodities. The spectacular aspect of religious ritual as exemplified by the monumental scale of the Yeha Temple would have served as a powerful magnet to surrounding populations.

All of these factors probably played a role in inducing such a large number of families within the Aksumite realm to settle at Enda Gully, eventually forming a town that accounted for some 50% of the estimated regional population based on sites actually studied. These are families that probably would have otherwise formed villages and hamlets throughout the Adua Basin and the Adua/Yeha Corridor—areas where a deficit of communities was noted.

The contemporaneity of South Arabian intrusion and the formation of the town of Enda Gully strongly suggests that the Early Pre-Aksumite population of the region surveyed continued to grow all during the period, and that there was only a modest resident population in the area prior to those events. But from wherever they might have come within the Aksumite *culture area* (i.e. northern Ethiopian Plateau country), the migrants were not from South Arabia or elsewhere outside the cultural region.

CHAPTER TWO
The Middle Pre-Aksumite Period

INTRODUCTION

The Middle Pre-Aksumite Period is a difficult one to interpret. On the one hand, there are numerous indications that a cultural break has been achieved between South Arabia and the cultural elite of the survey region. On the other hand, the process of population nucleation begun during the Early Pre-Aksumite Period continues, as does an apparent shift to greater and greater dependence upon irrigation agriculture.

The cultural break is often subtle, as in Francis Anfray's observation (1963) that the mortuary assemblage at Grat Abune Afsea exhibits aesthetic originality suggestive of a growing autonomy despite the continuing presence of South Arabian stylistic and conceptual traditions. Or the renovations documented for the Yeha Temple involving partial dismantlement of the original structure and the incorporation of masonry pieces containing South Arabian inscriptions as ordinary masonry fill.

Less subtle indications of a cultural break include the assessment by Anfray (1973b) that Grat Beal Gubri was converted from a religious shrine to an elite residential complex. The apparent abandonment of the South Arabian shrine at Abba Pentaleon, and the appearance of architecturally more modest shrines along the southern edge of the Aksumite Plateau such as Gobochela. Inscriptions in South Arabian script recovered at Gobochela indicate it was a shrine to the South Arabian god *Almuqah,* proprietary to a small number of lineage/clans of a single tribe (Drewes 1959).

But the most dramatic indication of a cultural shift is the decline of the Yeha Valley as the center of initiatives relating to population redeployment and political hegemony, and its replacement by a series of large, nucleated settlements along the southern periphery of the Aksumite Plateau: Enda Seglamen, Adi Atero, Melazo. Each of the above-mentioned communities appears to be associated with religious shrines and/or elite residences of masonry construction.

Still, it is not difficult to document the continuing importance of a South Arabian cultural framework within the Middle Pre-Aksumite Period. One need only point to inscriptions in South Arabian monumental script, the worship of the South Arabian deity *Almuqah,* the continuing operation of the Yeha Temple, and elite tombs containing grave goods fully within the stylistic canon of South Arabia, to make the case for a pervasive South Arabian cultural presence.

The circumstances described in the above paragraphs form the basis for postulating the continued presence of an

Ethio-Sabaean Elite—an indigenous elite that had been profoundly influenced by South Arabian culture but which had gradually transformed it over time. What has been referred to as the *Da'amat Kingdom* is believed to represent the political manifestation of this indigenous elite.

SETTLEMENT PATTERN

It is the shift in settlement pattern that holds the best clue to the nature of the changes that mark the Middle Pre-Aksumite Period. Two processes begun in the Early Pre-Aksumite Period come to completion during this period: (1) population nucleation, and (2) a growing dependence upon irrigation agriculture. Despite an almost doubling of the estimated overall population in the surveyed region, to almost 13,000 inhabitants, a remarkable 84% of that population can now be found in *towns* or *large villages* located in areas favorable for irrigation agriculture.

What is important, however, is the fact that these accomplishments were achieved by the establishment of three new political and population centers outside the Yeha Valley— Enda Seglamen, Adi Atero, Melazo—and one new population center inside the Yeha Valley (Hanza Moholita). The new one in the Yeha Valley—Hanza Moholita—replaces the town of Enda Gully and the village of Grat Abune Afsea, and in the process brings about a reduction in valley population from an estimated 3800 in the Early Pre-Aksumite Period to an estimated 2200 in the Middle Pre-Aksumite Period.

Thus the focus of nucleated population has shifted from the Yeha Valley to the southern edge of the Aksumite Plateau. Yet no single community stands out. Both Adi Atero and Enda Seglamen were large towns with resident populations estimated at 3400 and 4000 respectively. What this suggests is that some level of political decentralization had occurred among the *Ethio-Sabaean Elite*. Each of the three prominent communities along the south edge of the Aksumite Plateau—Enda Seglamen, Adi Atero, Melazo—seem to have had elite residences and religious sanctuaries; thereby duplicating the institutional features available at Yeha.

Irrigation agriculture of the sort identified for the Yeha Valley during the Early Pre-Aksumite Period appears now to have superceded the small-scale indigenous practices illustrated by the Mai Agazen Basin example given in the preceding chapter. What has been referred to as the *South Arabian* type, based on the impoundment and distribution of rain-fed stream runoff that maximizes the area under cultivation, now appears to provide the economic basis of these new large towns and villages along the southern edge of the Aksumite Plateau.

The special character of the settlements along the southern edge of the Aksumite Plateau is further reflected in the results of an analysis of the geographic distribution of diagnostic ceramic attributes. The reader will recall that during the Early Pre-Aksumite Period three subregional settlement groups could be defined by distribution of diagnostic ceramic attribute clusters:

Aksum Southwest, Aksum-Central, Adua-Yeha (see Figure 5). A comparable analysis for the Middle Pre-Aksumite Period reveals a newly configured *Aksum-Central* consisting of dispersed *hamlet* and *small village* settlements positioned to exploit the highly fertile soils of Ecozone I. Set off from *Aksum-Central* is the land along the southern edge of the Aksumite Plateau, newly termed *Aksum-South* consisting of *towns* and *large villages* adjacent to drainage systems suitable for South Arabian-style irrigation farming. The Valley of Yeha constitutes a third subregion, but one which shares some diagnostic ceramic attributes with *Aksum-South* (see Figure 6).

It appears that the Middle Pre-Aksumite Period accommodated two competing cultural systems. One consisted of an egalitarian population settled in *hamlets* and *small villages* in areas in which the richest soils could be farmed without recourse to irrigation. No religious shrines, elite dwellings, or elaborate tombs were associated with this group. This system dominated the central, northern, and western sectors of the Aksumite Plateau (*Aksum-Central*). The survey suggests that the population associated with this cultural system grew only modestly between the Early Pre-Aksumite Period and the end of the Middle Pre-Aksumite Period.

Most of the population growth noted earlier was associated with communities identified with the second cultural system, one that contained a small elite segment operating well within the cultural orbit of South Arabia. These are communities that tend to be *large villages* or *towns*, that occupy lands amenable to South Arabian-style irrigation farming, and that frequently contain or are in proximity to religious architecture, elite residences, or burials containing South Arabian-style artifacts. The subregions *Aksum-South* and *Yeha Valley* exemplify this cultural system.

But as pointed out at the beginning of the chapter, there is evidence that the cultural system exhibiting South Arabian affinity has already evolved in ways that suggest long-term *in situ* development. It does not appear that regular new infusions of South Arabian elites characterized this period. On the contrary, one suspects that the elites of Middle Pre-Aksumite communities are an indigenous group that continues to affirm South Arabian cultural norms but in a modified form.

The fact that substantial population growth is associated with this cultural system, a growth attributable to indigenous in-migration most probably, would suggest that this *Ethio-Sabaean Elite* continue to attract adherents to the areas they control—such as *Aksum-South*. However, if one were to attribute these developments to the *Da'amat Polity* discussed in the previous chapter, one would also have to observe that at least within the region under study the *Da'amat Polity* was undergoing significant decentralization during the Middle Pre-Aksumite Period.

A total of 22 residential communities, six special structures, and one cemetery are assigned to this period (see Figure 6). The estimated population for the areas actually surveyed has almost doubled when compared with the Early Pre-Aksumite Period. The population estimate for the Early Pre-Aksumite Period was about 7,000, while the estimate for the Middle Pre-Aksumite Period is about 13,000; an increase of about 80%. Despite this increase, the estimated population of the surveyed portion of the Yeha Valley System has dropped by about 40% to around 2200, while that of the southern drainage areas of the Aksumite Plateau has increased seven-fold to about 8000.

The Plain of Aksum and associated *ambas* of the Aksumite Plateau show only modest growth in estimated population (from about 1800 to about 2000). The Western Periphery of the Aksumite Plateau continues to have a negligible population, but the Northern Periphery now hosts a *large village*.

The Adua Basin area is difficult to estimate since it was not adequately sampled, particularly along the drainage systems of the basin proper. It is even possible that some significant fraction of the population reported in the Southern Drainage System may have come from the Adua Basin and the adjacent Adua-Yeha Corridor.

ECOLOGICAL OBSERVATIONS

Perhaps the most remarkable change associated with the Middle Pre-Aksumite Period was the relative decline in the prominence of Ecozones I and II. In the Early Pre-Aksumite

Period 75% of the estimated population occupied lands within these ecozones, but during the subsequent period the percentage drops to 34%. Ecozones I and II consist of *Welka A & B* soils derived from alkali olivine basalts that appear as black and brown clays respectively. They are regarded by the farmers interviewed as the premier soils of the region: highly fertile and requiring no fallowing cycles or fertilization.

A full two-thirds of the estimated population occupied lands within Ecozone V. The soil of Ecozone V is *Chincha Ba'akel B*, derived from limestone and dolomite and appearing as a brown sandy loam. Farmers report that this soil is fertile but requires intervention in the form of fallowing cycles or fertilization or both to sustain its productivity.

The population shift to Ecozone V can only be understood in the context of South Arabian style irrigation farming. The three large communities along the southern edge of the Aksumite Plateau—Enda Seglamen, Adi Atero, and Melazo—are all located on bluffs overlooking drainage basins that satisfy the requirements of micro-catchment irrigation. One of the basins—the Mai Agazen—was used in Chapter One to illustrate the type of small-scale, stream-fed irrigation that is believed to have been indigenous to the area. The point was made that with aggressive intervention, in the form of impoundment and canal features, it probably would have been possible to almost triple the area under irrigation. It was argued in Chapter One that maximising the area of irrigated farmlands by such aggressive intervention could be viewed as a hallmark of communities with strong South Arabian cultural affinities. The soils of the southern drainage systems of the Aksumite Plateau are Chincha Ba'akel B (i.e. Ecozone V). Thus, any coordinated shift from rain-fed cultivation to irrigation cultivation within the area of the Aksumite Plateau would inevitably involve a shift from premier to secondary soils.

It is important to note that the basin areas of the Adua Basin are within Ecozone V and do have irrigation potential that would appear to have been fully comparable to that of the Southern Drainage Systems of the Aksumite Plateau. Towns similar to Enda Seglamen and Adi Atero could well have existed but remain undetected due to inadequate sampling.

COMMUNITY PATTERNING

Despite the observed increase in estimated population, the number of communities in the surveyed area has declined by almost 37%: 35 to 22. This is the result of a reduction in the number of small communities—*hamlets* and *small villages*—from 31 to 15, and a consequent buildup of population within *large villages* and *towns*. In the Early Pre-Aksumite Period 29% of the estimated population in the surveyed area was associated with *hamlets* or *small villages*, while 71% were associated with *large villages* or *towns*. In the Middle Pre-Aksumite Period the percentages are 6% and 94% respectively, revealing a dramatic shift to large nucleated settlements.

There are two aspects of community patterning to be explored: the geographical distribution of communities (and their constituent populations as estimated) and the extent to which one can discern groupings of these communities that reflect the manner in which social and political factors have organized the regional population into spatially discrete subregions.

During the Middle Pre-Aksumite Period site density averages 0.11 sites per sq. km. Estimated population for this period based on an analysis of actually recorded sites averages 64 persons per sq. km. The following discussion points up just how widely each of the four principal physiograpic zones diverge from such benchmark averages.

The Aksumite Plateau area, taken as a whole, comes closest to approximating the figures given above, with 0.16 sites per sq. km. and 83 persons per sq. km. But if one excludes the Southern Drainage sub-area, the estimated population density of the Aksumite Plateau area drops dramatically to 20 persons per sq. km. This was because the Southern Drainage sub-area, comprising some 52 sq. km., contained most of the population—with an estimated density of 365 persons per sq. km.

No sites were detected in the Adua Basin area, despite the fact that 17% of its land surface was surveyed. Unfortunately, however, those areas within the Adua Basin where micro-catchment irrigation could have been practiced were not included in the sample surveyed. And only one site was detected in the Adua/Yeha Corridor.

The Yeha Valley System also only yielded one site, but this was a *small town* with an estimated population of over two thousand. Taken as a whole, the Yeha Valley System yielded an estimated population density of 117.2 persons per sq. km. But when just the *basins* sub-area—which can support micro-catchment irrigation—is considered, the estimated density rises sharply to 278.3 persons per sq. km.

It is clear that community patterning varied dramatically among physiographic areas within the region during the Middle Pre-Aksumite Period. As in the Early Pre-Aksumite Period, there was an apparent deficit in population in both the Adua Basin and the Adua/Yeha Corridor areas. A scenario similar to that put forward to explain this phenomenon in that earlier period would seem to apply here as well, namely that rural populations in these areas in particular gravitated to urban centers located elsewhere in the survey region. But, in contrast to the scenario put forward in the previous chapter—which had the rural population of the Adua Basin and the Adua/Yeha Corridor take up residence within the Yeha Valley System—one would guess that in this period the movement was mostly to the newly emergent towns of the Southern Drainage sub-area of the Aksumite Plateau.

Additional insight into the relationships between the sub-areas is given by consideration of ceramic variables and by the relative access sub-areas had to imported obsidian.

VESSEL DECORATIVE TREATMENT

All 724 sherds for which decorative treatment was in evidence were coded. As mentioned previously, the coding protocol contained 91 variants that represent a wide variety of decorative technique/design permutations. However, only 19 of the 91 variants were encountered among the Middle Pre-Aksumite assemblages. And, as in the Early Pre-Aksumite Period, two of the variants—*grooved [simple linear], grooved [complex linear]*—comprised a good portion of the sample (in this case 60%). Given their ubiquity throughout the survey region, they were of little help in the exercise at hand. Analysis thus rested upon the remaining 290 sherds and 17 decorative treatment variants.

An inspection of the distribution of the 17 variants within and between the principal physiographic areas of the survey region led to the identification of three which held some promise in defining subregional site groupings: (1) *fluted [vertical]*; (2) *punctated [round impression, simple design]*; (3) *incised [zone separation, punctate zone]*.

VESSEL LIP FORM

All 962 rim sherds collected were coded for lip form. The coding protocol contained 48 variants. Of those 48, 18 were never encountered. Among the remaining 30 variants, those that represented *unmodified* forms (i.e. LF 01 - LF 05) were so ubiquitous, and so numerous (comprising 77% of the sample), that they were of no use in this analysis. An inspection of the distribution of the remaining 25 lip form (LF) variants, among the principal physiographic areas of the survey region led to the identification of three which held promise in defining sub-regional site groupings: (1) *wedge [external]*; (2) *wedge [internal]*; (3) *labial flange [beveled]*.

The patterns resulting from the analysis are not as strong, nor do they involve as many traits, as in the Early Pre-Aksumite Period. A contrast between the settlements of *Aksum-Central* and those of *Aksum-South* is only modestly reflected in the contrasting incidence of three decorative treatments and two lip forms. However, the overlapping diagnostic trait (labial flange [beveled]) between *Aksum-South* and the Yeha Valley suggests a somewhat heightened level of interaction between these elite-dominated site groupings.

This idea of a closer link between *Aksum-South* and the Yeha Valley is further reinforced by the distribution pattern of obsidian artifacts. Among the 22 sites located on the Aksumite Plateau only those settlements located in the Southern Drainage System contain obsidian. The sites in question are Seglamen, Adi Atero, Melazo, Gobochela, and Melazo. Obsidian, however, was ubiquitous among sites in and around the Yeha Valley.

Given the proximity of the above-mentioned sites to other settlements on the Aksumite Plateau, the sharp contrast would seem to suggest that there was a politically contrived barrier between the two *sub-regions* on the Aksumite Plateau, and that furthermore, the communities within *Aksumite South* participated in an interaction sphere that included the Yeha Enclave. Accordingly, it seems reasonable to advance the notion that an ethnic, economic and political axis obtained between the Middle Pre-Aksumite Period sites of the Southern Drainage System of the Aksumite Plateau and those representing the population east of the Adua Basin.

CHAPTER THREE
The Late Pre-Aksumite Period

THE SOUTHERN PERIPHERY OF THE AKSUMITE PLATEAU

It would appear that early in the Late Pre-Aksumite Period the viability of large-scale irrigation systems in the southern periphery of the Aksumite Plateau was fatally compromised. What ecological or political factors were involved remains to be determined, but what is unmistakable is the fact that an estimated 8000 residents—densely packed into two *large towns* and one *large village*—abandon the area. These were the Middle Pre-Aksumite *towns* of Enda Seglamen and Adi Atero, and the *large village* of Melazo. The Southern Drainage Systems of the Aksumite Plateau appear largely bereft of inhabitants during the Late Pre-Aksumite Period.

This is not to say that this area was no longer agriculturally productive. In fact, all three above-mentioned communities were reestablished—albeit at a much smaller scale—during the subsequent Early Aksumite Period. But it is likely that these later inhabitants exploited the ecotonal aspect of the area as present-day farmers do: dry farming of the Ecozone I soils on the immediately adjacent Plain of Aksum, grazing livestock on the well-watered bottom lands of the southern drainage systems, and practicing various fertility interventions in support of the cultivation of the Ecozone V and VI soils in the latter area.

Our survey would suggest that the redeployment of that population did not involve either the remaining portions of the Aksumite Plateau or the hills and interconnecting basins of the Valley of Yeha. None of these areas exhibited extraordinary increases in population. And although there was an observed overall 44% reduction in population in the surveyed region to about 5700 inhabitants, owing to our inability to complete the scheduled survey of the Adua Basin and surrounding areas it is difficult to confidently evaluate what role, if any, that area played in absorbing some fraction of the dispossessed population. However, from an ecological standpoint the Adua basin and its eastern extensions closely resemble the bottomlands of the Adua-Yeha Corridor. Should the former area have been as lightly inhabited during the Middle Pre-Aksumite Period as can be documented for the latter area it could certainly have accommodated an infusion of new residents on a significant scale.

A significant population increase did occur, however, in the bottomlands of the Adua-Yeha Corridor. From an estimated 50 inhabitants or so in the Middle Pre-Aksumite Period the estimated population grew to over 1700 persons during the Late Pre-Aksumite Period based upon actual site documentation.

The fact that a key community in the corridor—Soheferes—is estimated to have been a *small town* with a nucleated population of almost 1300 persons offers support for the hypothesis that the source of this new infusion of resident population was some fraction of the dispossessed multitudes of the abandoned communities of Seglamen, Adi Ataro, and Melazo.

THE YEHA VALLEY

More was dispossessed than simply the inhabitants as the communities along the Southern Drainage System of the Aksumite Plateau were abandoned. The establishment of large nucleated communities supported by large-scale irrigation systems in the Southern Drainage section of the Aksumite Plateau during the Middle Pre-Aksumite Period is believed to have been sponsored and administered by elite cadres of the polity based in the Valley of Yeha. With the collapse of that system, and the consequent need to abandon the settlements dependent upon that system, it appears that the Yeha elite was discredited.

What one observes in the archaeological record of the Late Pre-Aksumite Period is a radical split between the redeployed population and the elite cadres that presumably once ruled those abandoned towns. The Valley of Yeha, the center of a polity (*Da'amat?*) that had been previously known for its South Arabian cultural affinities, exhibits no new influx of residential population. In fact, the *town* of Hanza Moholita continued to be the only significant settlement within the valley. But a dramatic new feature appeared on the landscape. In an arc along the foothills that form the edge of the valley, spaced at intervals of 1 to 2 kilometers, one observes multi-family elite residences having been built. Five such *elite residential complexes* have been documented. Three of the structures were built in solitary splendor, with no support community in their immediate vicinity. The other two were imbedded in *hamlet* or *small village* communities. All had panoramic views of the Valley of Yeha, and of the inescapable silhouette of the monumental remains of the Yeha Temple.

The special quality of this cluster of *elite residential complexes* cannot be overestimated. Only three other *elite residential structures* have been documented for this period—two on the summit of Bieta Giyorgis, and the other at the upper [east] end of the Adua-Yeha Corridor. Even in the previous period, at a time during which the polity within the Yeha Valley was prospering, only Grat Beal Gubri—that singular, *palace*-like structure that had previously been a religious shrine—could be regarded as an *elite residential complex*. It is this author's contention that some of the *elite residential complexes* encircling the Valley of Yeha represent a refugee community of elites that were dispossessed by the collapse of the Yeha-sponsored, irrigation-based settlement system along the southern periphery of the Aksumite Plateau.

THE ADUA-YEHA CORRIDOR

The Adua-Yeha Corridor appears to have been one of the areas in which the population that had abandoned the Southern Periphery of the Aksumite Plateau reestablished itself. Documentation for seven sites—one *small town*, two *small villages*, and four *hamlets*—accounts for the presence of an estimated 1700 new residents when compared to the previous period. The survey covered a good portion of the bottomlands and adjacent terraces of the corridor, and thus the above figure—albeit an estimate—would seem to constitute a comprehensive sample.

The dry farming potential of the broad basins to be found at various points along the corridor would certainly have been part of the attraction. But the corridor would also have seemed attractive to small communities that could disperse themselves throughout the rugged landscape, and that could take advantage of the strongly vertical ecotonal potential of the local ecology.

THE AKSUMITE PLATEAU

The survey documented the presence of one *large village*, six *small villages*, and four *hamlets* on the Aksumite Plateau during the Late Pre-Aksumite Period. Collectively, they comprised an estimated population of about 1300. These communities were fairly evenly dispersed over the plateau. Dry farming strategies, exploiting the rich dark soil of Ecozone I, appear to have been something that most of them had in common. With the exception of the communities on top of *Amba Bieta Giyorgis*, however, the immediate vicinity of historic Aksum appears not to have been a focus of settlement.

Although not part of the Pennsylvania State University Aksum-Yeha Regional Survey of 1974, recently discovered sites on *Amba Bieta Giyorgis* that appear to date to the Late Pre-Aksumite Period need to be introduced. Beginning in 1993, a joint archaeological expedition at *Bieta Giyorgis* (the hill (*amba*) immediately west of historic Aksum) was conducted by the Istituto Universitario Orientale, Naples (Italy) and Boston University (Fattovich et al: 2000).

Amba Bieta Giyorgis rises more than 150 meters above the surrounding plateau surface. A principal feature is a horseshoe-shaped, gently sloping plain called *Ona Nagast*. The entire summit of *Bieta Giyorgis* covers an area of about 3 square kilometers. The Penn State Survey recorded the existence of four sites on the summit, one of which dates to the Late Pre-Aksumite Period (Guadguad Agazien).

Careful stratigraphic excavation by the joint IUO-BU Expedition at two locations—Ona Enda Aboi Sewge and Ona Nagast—uncovered evidence of five architectural features that are reported to date to the Late Pre-Aksumite Period. They consist of the remains of two elite residential complexes, the remains of a domestic, non-elite structure at Ona Nagast, and two tombs at Ona Enda Aboi Sewge. In addition, a lithic workshop at Ona Nagast is also reported to be contemporary with the above sites. These sites will be referred to collectively as the "*Ona Nagast Complex*" in discussions at a later point in the chapter.

SUBREGIONAL SITE CLUSTERS

Archaeologists often speak of *Interaction Spheres* to describe clusters of communities that exhibit notable sets of shared attributes, particularly attributes that would have been the products of local exchange networks, or that reflect common inter-generational elements such as ceramic *micro-traditions*. Based upon data regarding the lithic and ceramic industries of Late Pre-Aksumite Period sites documented during this survey, there appear to have been *three* clusters of sites, or *Interaction Spheres*. And they correspond to the three geographical areas discussed above: the Yeha Valley, the Adua-Yeha Corridor, and the Aksumite Plateau.

OBSIDIAN DISTRIBUTION

Obsidian is a commodity famous for the vast distances over which it was traded during ancient times. The absence of such trade between closely spaced subregions therefore calls out for a political explanation. The reader will recall that among the sites located on the Aksumite Plateau during the Middle Pre-Aksumite Period, only those settlements located in the Southern Drainage System contained obsidian. It was precisely those communities that are believed to have been sponsored and governed by an elite cadre affiliated with the Yeha Enclave. The marked absence of obsidian among <u>all</u> other sites on the Aksumite Plateau suggests that during the Middle Pre-Aksumite Period simple geographic proximity was overridden by politically imposed boundaries with respect to obsidian trade.

Something quite similar occurred during the Late Pre-Aksumite Period, but the location of the obsidian trade barrier had shifted east. With the exception of Ser Ser Adi Keshi and Adi Islam, obsidian was recovered from <u>every site</u> east of the boundary depicted on Figure 7. In contrast, only <u>a single site</u> west of that boundary revealed obsidian despite a concerted effort to acquire specimens owing to their importance in the dating program.

This observation offers support for the hypothesis advanced earlier that a sizable fraction of the dispossessed communities of the southern periphery of the Aksumite Plateau were repatriated to what may have been their ancestral lands in the Adua Basin and in the Adua-Yeha Corridor. It also suggests the depth of the insularity between the indigenous population of the Aksumite Plateau and that of the subregions to the east.

JASPER DISTRIBUTION

One might legitimately argue that in the absence of obsidian local communities could make do with *jasper*, a type of stone that is locally available, abundant, and of high quality. Jasper, an aggregate of microgranular quartz and/or chalcedony is highly suitable for the production of cutting edge tools similar to obsidian. However, the pattern of distribution of jasper during the Late Pre-Aksumite Period makes it clear the situation is more complicated.

As Figure 7 illustrates, there is also a *Jasper Boundary*. All the sites west of that boundary—on both the Aksumite Plateau and within the Adua-Yeha Corridor—contained jasper artifacts. However, with the single exception of Sefra De Gezmati no sites east of the boundary contained jasper. East of the boundary, communities had to rely upon obsidian for their lithic cutting tools. This boundary is no less arbitrary than the *Obsidian Boundary*, for—as in the case of obsidian—jasper was also a widely traded commodity in certain parts of the ancient world.

But it is the cluster of sites in the Adua-Yeha Corridor that is particularly relevant to the issue in question: namely, whether the apparent barriers to obsidian trade were in fact simply a lack of demand. With the single exception of Adi Islam, all of the sites between the *Obsidian Boundary* and the *Jasper Boundary* (eight in number) contained <u>both</u> obsidian and jasper artifacts. It is unlikely that the jasper used to produce artifacts at these sites was secured through trade with communities on the Aksumite Plateau, for one would then expect a reciprocal exchange of obsidian for jasper. But what is certain is that all of the obsidian found at these sites was secured through trade, since the known geological sources of Ethiopian obsidian were some considerable distance away. The ubiquitous presence of both lithic materials among all of these sites would suggest that Late Pre-Aksumite Period communities of the Aksum-Yeha Survey Region preferred access to both obsidian and jasper, and thus the absence of one or the other would seem to require a political explanation.

The *Jasper Boundary* suggests that the communities east of the Adua Basin formed at least two distinct interaction spheres: a Yeha Valley site cluster and those sites south and southwest of the Yeha Valley. The reader will recall that earlier in this chapter the argument was made that there was a radical split between the dispossessed populations of the southern periphery of the Aksumite Plateau and the elite cadres that governed those large towns and villages. If the hypothesis is correct that the population in abandoning the southern periphery reclaimed what may have been their ancestral lands in the Adua-Yeha Corridor (among other areas) while the dispossessed elite sought refuge in the Yeha Valley, then the *Jasper Boundary* makes perfect sense, in political terms.

CERAMIC MICRO-TRADITIONS

The *Interaction Spheres*, or subregional groupings, of the Late Pre-Aksumite Period that emerged from a consideration of obsidian and jasper distributions can be further refined by consideration of two sets of ceramic variables: *Vessel Decorative Treatment (DT)* and *Vessel Lip Form (LF)*. These are attribute domains that are believed to reflect local exchange networks and/or inter-generational stylistic traditions.

VESSEL DECORATIVE TREATMENT

All 403 sherds recovered from Late Pre-Aksumite assemblages where decorative treatment was in evidence were coded. However, only 16 of the 90 possible variants were encountered among the Late Pre-Aksumite assemblages. The 16 variants can with some exceptions be grouped into *incised, grooved,* and *punctate* categories.

One of the first observations that gains the analyst's attention is the wide disparity in the number of sherds possessing decorative treatments among the three subregional site groupings identified above. The seven sites that comprise the Adua-Yeha Corridor grouping [including Sohoferes, which involved a *controlled* surface collection of over 1300 sherds] yielded only four sherds that possessed decorative treatment. And the Yeha Valley grouping, despite the presence of *five elite residential complexes* and a *small town*, only yielded 30 sherds that possessed decorative treatment. In contrast, the ten sites within the central part of the Aksumite Plateau—consisting mostly of *hamlets* and *villages*—yielded a total of 297 sherds possessing decorative treatment.

A largely concomitant byproduct of such disparity in the number of sherds possessing decorative treatment is the wide disparity in the *number* of decorative treatments represented within each of the three subregional site groupings. The Adua-Yeha Corridor contained three decorative treatments, the Yeha Valley grouping contained eight, whereas the sites in the central part of the Aksumite Plateau contained 15.

When one focuses upon the principal decorative treatment categories—*incised* and *grooved*—one observes that there is no appreciable difference in the occurrence of sherds exhibiting decorative treatments that fall within the *grooved* category between the Yeha Valley site group and the Central Aksum group (47% vs 39% respectively). However, the two groupings contrast significantly in the occurrence of decorative treatments that fall within the *incised* category. A full 54% of all decorated sherds in the Central Aksum group fall within the *incised* category, while only 27% of the decorated sherds in the Yeha Valley group fall within that category. The Adua-Yeha Corridor site grouping cannot be compared since it contained so few decorated sherds.

The three subregional site groupings can also be compared with respect to three specific *Decorative Treatment* attributes:

(1) *deep, wide, simple curvilinear incising;* (2) *shallow, narrow, simple linear incising;* (3) *complex linear grooving.* All three are revealed as diagnostic of the Aksum Central site grouping. No specific *Decorative Treatment* is diagnostic of either the Adua-Yeha Corridor grouping or the Yeha Valley grouping.

In addition to augmenting the basis upon which the three subregional site groupings can be differentiated, consideration of *Decorative Treatment* has also revealed that five of the 29 Late Pre-Aksumite sites fall outside all three of the site groupings: the two sites named Tareta, located on the Western Periphery of the Aksumite Plateau, and Hasina, located on the Northern Periphery of the Aksumite Plateau. All three sites fail to exhibit any of the three diagnostic attributes of the Aksum Central grouping. Conversely, the hamlets of Assi and Adi Islam—both located in the valley south of Yeha—exhibit a greater number of decorated sherds, and a greater variety of decorative treatments, than sites forming the neighboring Adua-Yeha Corridor group.

VESSEL LIP FORM

All 828 rim sherds collected were coded for lip form. An inspection of the distribution of the lip form (LF) variants among the subregional groupings under discussion led to the identification of three that can be considered diagnostic. They include LF47 (*external wedge*), LF80 (*horizontal labial flange*), and LF81 (*beveled labial flange*).

LF47 (*external* wedge) was diagnostic of *Aksum Central* in the Middle Pre-Aksumite Period, and it continued to be associated with that area during the Late Pre-Aksumite Period as well.

Particularly revealing is the presence of LF81 as a diagnostic of the Yeha Valley site grouping. The reader will recall that *beveled labial flange* was a diagnostic element for both the *Aksum-South* and the Yeha Valley site groupings during the Middle Pre-Aksumite Period. The fact that it continues to be associated with the Yeha Valley in the Late Pre-Aksumite Period is analogous to the pattern we observed with respect to obsidian distribution. As such, it strengthens the argument that the large-scale communities along the southern periphery of the Aksumite Plateau during the Middle Pre-Aksumite Period were linked culturally, economically, and politically to the polity that was based in the Yeha Valley.

And the fact that *Aksum-Central* showed continuity in its ceramic micro-tradition in the transition between the Middle Pre-Aksumite and Late Pre-Aksumite Periods further supports the demographic evidence that the abandonment of the large communities along the southern periphery of the Aksumite Plateau at the end of the Middle Pre-Aksumite Period did not affect the cultural landscape of *Aksum-Central*.

The five sites that on the basis of ceramic decorative treatment were excluded from membership in any of the three subregional site groupings (Tareta, Tareta, Hasina, Assi, and Adi Islam) remain separate from those groupings when consideration is also given to lip form morphology. Neither of the Tareta sites share LF47 with the *Aksum-Central* group, and Tareta (41-15-093) has a singular concentration of sherds of LF49. Only *unmodified* lip forms were recovered from the site of Hasina, setting it off from the sites of *Aksum-Central*. Adi Islam and Assi exhibited lip form diagnostics common to both the Yeha Valley (LF80/81) and to *Aksum-Central* (LF47), thereby disqualifying for membership in the Adua-Yeha Corridor group.

SETTLEMENT PATTERN SUMMARY

A new feature to appear during the Late Pre-Aksumite Period was the emergence of multiple *elite residential complexes*. Only one was believed to have existed during the Middle Pre-Aksumite Period—the refurbished Grat Beal Gubri. No fewer than eight are reported for the Late Pre-Aksumite Period (including the two at Ona Nagast). One may legitimately argue that they represent a secularized political leadership cadre. The variation in the size of these structures seems to have less to do with the hierarchical status of the respective elite families (all seem to fall within the *small* category of *elite structure*—up to 2000 sq. meters) than to the relative need to accommodate support staff within the walls of the structure rather than in an adjacent *hamlet* or *village*.

Concomitant with the appearance of *elite residential complexes* was the disappearance of religious structures—both shrines and temples. And even the elaborate tomb-based stelae at OAZ on Bieta Giyorgis, reported by the BU-IUO Joint Expedition would seem to have more to do with the mortuary celebration of a particular historic personality [a chief?] than with the adoration of any particular deity.

There was no significant difference in the percentage of the estimated population that resided in *hamlets* in the transition from the Middle to the Late Pre-Aksumite Period—from 2% to 3%. But there was a large increase the number of persons inhabiting *small villages*—from 4% to 25% of the total population. *Small Towns* also acquire greater prominence, accounting for some 61% of the Late Pre-Aksumite population. The big decline was in *large towns*: the percentage of the total estimated population residing in that type of community dropped from 58% to 0%. And *Large Villages* also witnessed a decline in relative importance.

POLITICAL ANALYSIS

The Late Pre-Aksumite Period witnessed a series of transformations, most of which have received some discussion already. The initial event appears to have been the abandonment of the *large towns* along the southern periphery of the Aksumite Plateau, and the likely redeployment of some of the estimated 8000 persons into the bottomlands of the Adua Basin and of the Adua-Yeha Corridor. Where possible, such as in the case of Soheferes, the dispossessed settlements retained cohesive communities of significant scale. But given the apparent choice of physiographic setting—narrow bottomlands often surrounded by rugged terrain with strong vertical relief—*small villages* and *hamlets* would often have been the most likely settlement solution. *Small villages* and *hamlets* also dominate the settlement pattern of the Aksumite Plateau.

No evidence of defensive deployment of settlements exists for this period, which seems to rule out inter-subregional hostilities of a scale that could account for the absence of economic contact. It is more likely that a combination of factors were at play. To begin with, the irresistible draw of spectacular religious ritual—of the sort that is exemplified by the presence of the Yeha Temple during the Early Pre-Aksumite Period—was no longer operative. *Ethio-Sabaean* religious institutions—shrines and temples—had been all but abandoned by the beginning of the Late Pre-Aksumite Period. Secondly, subregional market systems, of the sort documented for the ethnographic present would most likely have been in existence, facilitating local trade in the kind of commodities and goods that would have been essential to domestic life. As such, there would have been little incentive to visit neighboring markets. And finally, political affiliations—through the interconnections of village headman—and political feuds—such as the ones that probably account for the *Obsidian* and *Jasper Boundaries*—could account for the apparent unwillingness of villagers in close proximity to neighboring markets to utilize them.

What seems clear is that whatever political institutions obtained during this period they were of a scale too modest to bridge the parochial interests that are reflected in the apparent constraints to intra-subregional trade, but sufficiently robust to account for the existence of the three interaction spheres, or subregional groupings of sites.

THE ADUA-YEHA CORRIDOR SUBREGIONAL GROUPING

The key to a solution would appear to lie in the presence of an elite, multi-room residential complex at the site of Daro Atem. Strategically positioned on a promontory overlooking the eastern end of the Adua-Yeha Corridor, one can reasonably hypothesize that it represents the residence of an individual who has acquired the institutional trappings of political leadership among the population of the Corridor. In anthropological parlance, such an entity would be referred to as a *local chiefdom*.

For purposes of this study, a *local chiefdom* can be defined as one or more residential communities that occupy a physiographically well-defined landscape, and that are associated with at least one special masonry structure that has been provisionally identified as an *elite residential complex*.

The *Corridor Chiefdom* was a remarkably insular political entity. Despite the fact that a substantial proportion of its population resided in a single *small town*, the paucity of decorative treatments and of *modified* lip forms among the thousands of pottery sherds recovered from the seven settlements of this grouping give it the flavor of an isolated, utilitarian society. Perhaps the fact that the communities comprising this group tended to be located in bottomlands surrounded by steep, rugged mountains that form the Adua-Yeha Corridor had an impact on its material-culture aesthetics.

But despite the appearance of cultural isolation, the presence of imported obsidian at every site within the *chiefdom* demonstrates a link to the outside world, although most likely in the guise of itinerant traders who would periodically visit the settlements or attend the local market.

As mentioned earlier, interaction with communities in the adjacent Yeha Valley appears to have been severely constrained, as evidenced by the jasper boundary. A political explanation has been put forward: that the Adua-Yeha Corridor communities originated out of the dispossessed population of the southern periphery of the Aksumite Plateau, and that the discredited *elites* that had once ruled them had taken refuge within the Yeha Valley.

THE YEHA VALLEY SUBREGIONAL GROUPING

The Yeha Valley, with the remains of its monumental *ethio-sabaean* temple silhouetted against the sky, and its valley floor forming what was probably the last large-scale irrigation system in the region, evoked a cultural tradition that had been ascendant for centuries but which by Late Pre-Aksumite times had been largely eclipsed.

The *town* of Hanza Moholita appears not to have been affected by the transition from Middle Pre-Aksumite to Late Pre-Aksumite times. With its estimated 2200 inhabitants, it comprised almost the entirety of the population of the valley. It would have supplied the workforce to maintain the large-scale irrigation system that is believed also to have survived the transition.

The managerial cadre, consisting of elite families linked to the *ethio-sabaean* legacy of the valley, appears to have been significantly augmented by the arrival of refugee *elites* from the abandoned *towns* along the southern periphery of the Aksumite Plateau. Their monumental masonry residences formed an arc of settlement at the base of the hills starting at the north and extending around the eastern perimeter of the valley to a point due south.

Although apparently constrained in its economic and social interaction with local populations to the west, the presence of obsidian at all sites in the valley suggests that there was an opening for long distance trade to the east.

Did the Yeha Valley polity attempt to conserve at least some of the traditions of the earlier era despite the isolation it had to endure from communities in neighboring subregions? Only systematic excavation of one or more of the *elite residential complexes* will let us know for certain. But if settlement pattern data from the Early Aksumite Period is any indication, by the end of the Late Pre-Aksumite Period the Yeha Valley itself ceased to retain the importance it had previously enjoyed.

THE AKSUMITE PLATEAU SUBREGIONAL GROUPING

The population on the Aksumite Plateau was settled in *villages* and *hamlets* that were spread somewhat evenly across the landscape. But high on top of *Amba Bieta Giyorgis*, a landmark prominently visible to residents of the Plain of Aksum, were the elite residential and mortuary remains of the *Ona Nagast Complex*.

The *Ona Nagast Complex* consisted of two *elite residential complexes*, a supporting community of indeterminate size, a lithic workshop, and two elite tombs (Fattovich 1998, Fattovich et al 2000). All of these elements were located on *Amba Bieta Giyorgis*—the summit of which covers an area of about three square kilometers.

The profile given above warrants classifying the Aksumite Plateau Subregional Group as another example of the emergence of *local chiefdoms* during the Late Pre-Aksumite Period—one that we might wish to refer to as the *Aksumite Chiefdom*.

But the *Aksumite Chiefdom* was wholly unlike its contemporary—the *Corridor Chiefdom*—with respect to external contacts. Imported materials recovered from excavations within the *Ona Nagast Complex* reveal contacts with kingdoms along the Nile River—from Upper Nubia to Egypt (Fattovich et al 2000:24). It would therefore appear that the *Aksumite Chiefdom* played a key role in sponsoring and administering trade relationships that extended to the northwest as far as the Nile Valley, thereby providing a conduit for the export of locally available products.

Evidence for the economic impact of the trading role played by the leadership of the *Aksumite Chiefdom* was encountered at the *small village* of Adi Kerni. On the southern edge of the village was an area about one hectare in size that represented the remains of a factory-scale workshop, consisting of a substantial concentration of jasper artifacts. In addition to the usual debris of the lithic reduction process—flake detritus and core residues—a tool kit consisting mainly of thumbnail scraper planes and side scrapers dominated the assemblage.

Although experiments need to be conducted to confirm or disconfirm it, it is this author's opinion that a factory-scale workshop that featured principally *thumbnail scraper planes* was one that specialized in the processing of elephant ivory tusks and rhinoceros horn. The cracked and discolored surface of a tusk would most likely respond to such a tool, permitting the removal of such imperfections while at the same time creating a smooth, seamless finish that would enhance the value and marketability of the finished product. In fact, Laurel Phillipson of the British Archaeological Team that conducted excavations at Aksum in the 1990's reports that such scrapers (called *"Gudit Scrapers"* by her) produced planing marks on soft wood and soft stone that matched similar marks found on steatite seals and on worked ivory recovered from Late Aksumite deposits at Aksum (Phillipson 2000:439).

The scale of the industrial undertaking at Adi Kerni would seem to have required a fairly robust trade infrastructure, with locally based leadership that exhibited a strong entrepreneurial character.

THE AKSUMITE CHIEFDOM VS THE AKSUMITE KINGDOM

The earliest historical reference to the Aksumites is to be found in the *Periplus of the Erythraean Sea*, which is dated to the latter half of the 1st Century AD, and thus refers to the Late Pre-Aksumite Period. The unknown author of the text refers *"...to the city of the people called Aksumites..."* (Schoff 1912). His reference to the Aksumites was in the context of trade in elephant ivory and rhinoceros horn. Mention is made of the assembling of ivory and horn from the interior by the Aksumites and its subsequent distribution to trading centers closer to the Red Sea coast, such as Matara (Coloe) and Adulis.

Given the archaeological record as currently documented, it would be reasonable to assume that the *city* referred to in the

Periplus was the *Ona Nagast Complex*. Although not a city in demographic terms, the impact of the wealth and cultural influences that derived from long distance trade such as the construction of elaborate tombs, the erection of funerary stelae, the display of exotic treasures, and the erection of monumental edifices at the edge of the *amba's* escarpment, might quite reasonably have earned the *Ona Nagast Complex* the sobriquet of *city*.

As we will see in the next chapter, the *Ona Nagast Complex* becomes an integral component of the architectural and demographic complex of historic Aksum—the capital of the *Aksumite Kingdom*. But it is useful to preserve the separate identity of the *Ona Nagast Complex* during the period currently under study, for it permits us to appreciate the distinction between two significantly different phases of Aksumite political organization: *Chiefdom* and *Kingdom*.

From an archaeological standpoint, the distinction rests in the geographic extent of political integration. The *local chiefdom*, as we have defined it, consists of one or more communities that occupy a well-defined physiographic setting, and in which there is located an archaeologically recognizable *elite residential complex*. An additional—although not indispensable—element would be evidence of a ceramic micro-tradition that ties the aggregate of communities together in what we have referred to as an *interaction sphere*. That element is present with respect to the *Aksumite Chiefdom* of the Late Pre-Aksumite Period.

A *kingdom*, on the other hand, would emerge when there is credible archaeological evidence that a *chiefdom* has achieved political hegemony over one or more *local chiefdoms*. It would thereby become a regional or even an interregional political entity. The archaeological evidence obtained by the Penn State Aksum-Yeha Survey, and discussed in this chapter, would argue strongly against the notion that the *Aksumite Chiefdom* enjoyed political hegemony over neighboring *local chiefdoms*. Accordingly, it would be inappropriate to regard the *Aksumite* political entity of the Late Pre-Aksumite Period as a *kingdom*.

But evidence to be presented in the next chapter is compatible with the hypothesis that the leadership residing at the *Ona Nagast Complex* is transformed from governing a *chiefdom* during the Late Pre-Aksumite Period to governing a *kingdom* at the onset of the Early Aksumite Period. Despite this notion of a somewhat rather seamless link between the leadership of the *Ona Nagast Complex* and the leadership of the *Aksumite Kingdom*, it is culture-historically useful to regard the two phases as distinct, and to reflect that distinction in the terminology we use to refer to those phases.

The period of time during which the Aksumites exhibit the political configuration of a *local chiefdom* should, this author believes, be regarded as the final episode of the *Pre-Aksumite Era*. The argument derives from the fact that the Aksumites known in historical literature were, with the single exception of the *Periplus*, Aksumites that demonstrably exercised political hegemony over large areas of northern Ethiopia, and could with no difficulty be characterized as a *kingdom*. In this sense, the *Pre-Aksumite Era* was the era preceding the emergence of the *Aksumite Kingdom*, as herein defined.

CHAPTER FOUR
The Early Aksumite Period

INTRODUCTION

The Early Aksumite Period was a particularly dynamic one. It is the period during which the Aksumite Kingdom was established—a process that transformed elite and non-elite residential patterns, inter-subregional contacts, and a host of other elements of culture in the survey region. In consequence, the single culture-historical snapshot, comprising several centuries, which a chapter like this purports to provide is somewhat less than satisfactory. But with the aid of insights provided by recent research on *Amba Bieta Giyorgis* by IUO/BU archaeologists, an attempt will be made to remedy that situation by the reconstruction a two-phase process within the period.

But before we begin the political analysis, a basic summary of Early Aksumite Period settlement data is in order. A total of 52 sites are believed to date to the Early Aksumite Period. Although most are sites that were originally documented by the Penn State Archaeological Survey of 1974, a significant number are sites that were originally discovered and reported on by other archaeologists—going back to the 1906 German Expedition, and extending up to the present-day IUO/BU Expedition. Whenever possible, an effort has been made to integrate these sites into the analytical framework of the present study—either by revisiting the sites and taking samples, or by interpreting the previously published site descriptions in a manner that makes them intelligible in terms of the comprehensive settlement pattern emerging from this study.

Of course, not all of the 52 sites were residential in nature. Included in the total number were six stone quarries exploited in the production of stelae and dressed masonry stone, five stelae fields that served as mortuary precincts for the elite, two religious shrines or sanctuaries, one collection of commemorative stone thrones, and one factory-scale workshop.

SUBREGIONAL INTERACTION SPHERES
JASPER & OBSIDIAN DISTRIBUTION

The *Jasper* and *Obsidian Boundaries* that occurred during the Late Pre-Aksumite Period disappear during the Early Aksumite Period. Both lithic materials have regional distribution. In fact, one of the largest concentrations of obsidian artifacts encountered dating to this period was observed at the site of Adi Quatia—right in the heart of Aksum. The reader will recall that in the previous period obsidian was to be found at only one site west of the Adua-Yeha Corridor.

CERAMIC MICRO-TRADITIONS

The relaxation of subregional constraints on interaction that was evidenced by the disappearance of lithic distribution boundaries is also reflected in part in the ceramic data. Rather than multiple, discrete interaction spheres, such as those that appeared during the Late Pre-Aksumite Period, only a single *Ceramics Boundary* obtains within the Early Aksumite Period. The boundary separates the Aksumite Plateau from all subregions to the east [within the survey region]. But within each of the two major subregions, all constituent physiographic zones share a common ceramic micro-tradition—this, despite evidence to be presented later in this chapter that multiple political entities populated each of the two subregions.

VESSEL DECORATIVE TREATMENT (DT)

All 320 sherds recovered from Early Aksumite assemblages for which decorative treatment was in evidence were coded. Only 18 of the 90 possible variants were encountered among the Early Aksumite assemblages. The 18 variants can with some exceptions be grouped into *incised, grooved, punctate,* and *fluted* categories.

The wide disparity in numbers of decorated sherds and in the variety of decorative treatments that was so notable in the Late Pre-Aksumite Period between the Aksumite Plateau and the subregions to the east has also disappeared. Sites in the

Adua-Yeha subregion contained 26% of all decorated sherds, and exhibited 13 of the 18 DT variants.

For one principal category of decorative treatment, for which there were three variants—*grooved linear*—there was no appreciable difference between the two subregions. The Aksumite Plateau possessed 58% of such sherds, while the Adua-Yeha subregion possessed 42%. And 73% sites throughout the survey region exhibited one or another of those variants.

But with respect to three other categories—*incised, fluted,* and *punctate*—the two subregions contrasted significantly. Variants of all three categories serve as diagnostic ceramic traits of the Aksumite Plateau population during this period, and thereby define an Aksumite Plateau Ceramic Micro-Tradition.

VESSEL LIP FORM (LF)

All 971 rim sherds collected were coded for lip form. Among the 48 possible lip forms, there were three variants of *Thickened With Taper* that appeared to be moderately diagnostic of the subregions east of the Aksumite Plateau. But the two subregions did share substantial resemblances with respect to *wedge variants* and *labial flange variants*. The reader will recall that *labial flange variants* were diagnostic of the Yeha Valley Enclave during the Late Pre-Aksumite Period.

POLITICAL ANALYSIS

As mentioned earlier, this period is enormously dynamic. Multiple time segment snapshots would be needed to do it justice. Unfortunately, given the limitations of a regional surface survey only a single multi-century snapshot can be produced. However, insights emerging from the excavation of one of the six *elite residential structures* at Ona Nagast by archaeologists from Boston University and the Istituto Universitario Orientale in Naples, Italy, permit us to glimpse some of the details of a more dynamic picture. And in consequence, this author feels emboldened to analytically reconstruct a two-phase sequence within the period—a sequence that appears to make more intelligible the complex settlement pattern of the Early Aksumite Period.

THE ONA NAGAST COMPLEX

The IUO/BU Expedition encountered the remains of an *elite residential complex* within what is known as the Ona Nagast archaeological complex. The Ona Nagast Complex is located in the southwest sector of *Amba Bieta Giyorgis*, and on the ridge and [NE facing] terraced slopes that lead down to the Mai Lahlaha streambed. The complex has a floor plan comparable to that of the *palace* structures described elsewhere in this chapter, but significantly smaller in scale. The complex appears to be one of approximately six such *elite residential structures* that formed a tight cluster along the Ona Nagast ridge.

Fattovich et al (2000:27) suggest that perhaps there is a connection between the abandonment of the Ona Nagast *elite residential complex* [by the elites] and the beginning of *palace* construction at Aksum proper—i.e. at the south end of the Mai Hejja Valley, located between *Amba Bieta Giyorgis* and *Amba Mai Qoho*. The assumption being that Ona Nagast was the original political center of the emergent Aksumite Kingdom during the *Early Phase* of the Early Aksumite Period. Subsequently, the capital was relocated down at the base of the eastern slopes of *Amba Bieta Giyorgis*—in and around the Mai Hejja Valley. One might wish to regard that transition as the *Late Phase* of the Early Aksumite Period.

Provisional acceptance of the thesis put forward by Fattovich et al (*ibid*) allows us to view the settlement history of the Early Aksumite Period as a two-phase sequence: an *Early Phase* prior to the establishment of Aksum as a capital, and a *Late Phase* during which the capital of Aksum dominates the settlement pattern of the survey region.

THE *EARLY PHASE* OF THE EARLY AKSUMITE PERIOD

Even before the establishment of Aksum as the capital of the newly emergent Aksumite Kingdom, the *surveyed* portions of the Aksum-Yeha Region experienced a doubling of the resident population—from about 5,700 in the Late Pre-Aksumite Period to about 11,000 in the current period. Many were residents of the three *towns* located east of the Plain of Aksum, but an appreciable number were widely distributed among the many *hamlets* and *villages* to be found throughout the survey region. There was no apparent concentration of population in the immediate vicinity of the Ona Nagast Complex, if one views the two towns in the Mai Hejja Valley as components of the later Aksumite capital.

But perhaps the most remarkable feature of the *Early Phase* of the Early Aksumite Period was the proliferation of *elite residential complexes* across the survey region. As illustrated in Figure 9, Ona Nagast was not the only location where new *elite residential structures* were being built at the outset of the period.

Nine *elite residential precincts* are documented (see Figure 9). Five of them resemble Ona Nagast in having multiple structures within a single precinct. The relative scale of the elite complexes is difficult to ascertain since no secure estimates of size are available for three of the key precincts: Ona Nagast, Seglamen, and Gobochelo-Melazo. Accordingly, one cannot yet assert that the Ona Nagast Complex was qualitatively different *in architectural scale* from the other two, or indeed from a number of the other elite precincts. Thus, despite provisional acceptance of the notion that the Ona Nagast leadership formed the basis for Aksumite kingship, the kingdom in its *earliest phase* most likely involved the participation of leadership cadres imbedded within polities geographically dispersed within the survey region, and fully comparable organizationally.

Joseph W. Michels

TRADITIONAL SUBREGIONAL MARKETS AS A CLUE TO LOCAL CHIEFDOM BOUNDARIES

A clue as to what these polities might have looked like geographically has its source in the mapped outline of the subregional market system of 1974 produced in connection with the Penn State regional study. Using the *elite residential precincts* as key nodes, and then superimposing the ethnographically documented subregional market system of 1974 onto the regional map, the basic outlines of what this author chooses to call *local chiefdoms* come into focus. Figure 10 illustrates the nine *local chiefdoms* that can ultimately be configured. Geographical names have been attached to each polity for the sake of convenience.

The application of the mapped parameters of the 1974 subregional market system makes intelligible the distribution of the nine *elite residential precincts*. The three closely spaced precincts at the eastern edge of the survey region can by analogy be understood as forming the boundaries that separated communities whose residents attended the Yeha Market, the Adua Market, and the Faras Mai Market respectively. Archaeologically, those same boundaries help define the *Yeha Valley Chiefdom,* the *Corridor Chiefdom,* and the *Southern Valley Chiefdom.*

And the boundaries that separate communities within each of the market spheres of the Aksum Market, the Wukro Market, and the Mehara Dagou Market help, archaeologically, to define the *Aksumite Chiefdom,* the *Western Periphery Chiefdom*, and the *Mai Agazen Chiefdom* respectively.

The subregional market boundary separating the Aksum Market from the Adua Market can be applied to help differentiate the *Western Hills Chiefdom* from the *Adua Basin Chiefdom*. And if one considers the *ceramic boundary* discussed earlier in this chapter it is possible to locate the boundary separating the *Western Hills Chiefdom* from the *Aksumite Chiefdom*.

The only chiefdom boundary not independently supported by either ethnographic analogy or ceramic analysis is that between the *Adua Basin Chiefdom* and the *Corridor Chiefdom*. Here one must rely on precedent. The boundaries of the *Corridor Chiefdom* were clearly established by ceramic analysis during the Late Pre-Aksumite Period (see Figure 8). If one assumes that the *Corridor Chiefdom* boundaries remained stable in the transition to the Early Aksumite Period, then the boundary between it and the *Adua Basin Chiefdom* becomes clear.

What seems most likely is that the emergence of the Aksumite Kingdom at the beginning of the Early Aksumite Period involved more than simply an architectural makeover of the Ona Nagast enclave on *Amba Bieta Giyorgis*. It must have also involved the establishment of local polities [chiefdoms] across the survey region (and beyond) that resembled Ona Nagast both organizationally and territorially. One must conclude that the Aksumite Kingdom during the *Early Phase* of the Early Aksumite Period consisted of an aggregate of local chiefdoms, most likely organized as a confederacy, with the *Aksumite Chiefdom* serving in a paramount role.

THE *LATE* PHASE OF THE EARLY AKSUMITE PERIOD

From an analytical standpoint, the *Late Phase* of the Early Aksumite Period is marked by the establishment of the site of Aksum (see Figure 11). A consideration of the range of architectural and settlement features that constitute the site offers us a useful place to begin in an assessment of the political significance of this development.

TOWNS AT AKSUM

There are 2 towns within the confines of Aksum, estimated collectively to have accommodated about 6,000 inhabitants. They are positioned at the northern and western perimeters (respectively) of the Central Mortuary Precinct.

A third town is hinted at in the archaeological record of the Daro Addi Kilte precinct located north of the Gondar/Adua Highway and west of the Mai Lahlaha riverbed. The remains of a multi-room structure underlying the Middle Aksumite Dongour *palace*, and Unit 2 of Puglisi's *sondage*, together with Anfray's *sondages* (Anfray 1972a) east and north of the Dongour *palace* all offer the intriguing possibility that an Early Aksumite town perhaps as large as 10 hectares might exist in that precinct.

PALACES AT AKSUM

There are six *palaces* in an around Aksum. For the purposes of this study, a *palace* is define as an elite residential complex comprising an area of 2000 sq. meters or larger. Five are clustered together at the southern end of the Mai Hejja Valley, and thereby form what can be called a *palace precinct*. The sixth *palace* is located a short distance east of the northern end of the Mai Hejja Valley. No *elite residential structures* smaller than a *palace* were identified within the confines of the site. The six *palace* structures of Aksum are estimated to have collectively accommodated close to 2000 additional residents. Archeological investigations and architectural reconstructions of such sites suggest that these multi-storied complexes provided elaborate residential cores for elite households, living space for a variety of retainers, warehouse space for commodities, and public space for the conduct of business.

MORTUARY PRECINCTS AT AKSUM

A Central Mortuary District, consisting of the Main Stelae Field and the Northern Stelae Field, is located at the center of the Mai Hejja Valley. Additional mortuary precincts were to be found east and west of the southern end of the valley—the Eastern Stelae Field and the Gudit Stelae Field, respectively. Two other mortuary precincts dating to this period—the Bieta Giyorgis Stelae Field and the Medoque Stelae Field—were located away from the site of Aksum, and thus do not directly figure in any portrait of the capital itself.

Each mortuary precinct consisted of the entombed remains of elite personages. Each vertically installed stone monolith often marked several such burials. The monoliths were of varying size and quality of finish. The largest and most elaborately decorated monoliths [or stelae] were to be found—in most cases—in the Central Mortuary District at the heart of the capital of Aksum. Excavations also suggest that the most elaborately constructed subterranean tombs were also to be found in those locations. Current published accounts place the number of stelae among the four mortuary precincts of Aksum at greater than 700. Only a small fraction are fully *dressed* monoliths, and of those, only about 10 are decorated. All the rest are irregular, *roughed out*, monoliths of locally available stone.

The relative centrality of the precincts, the varying elaborateness of the subterranean tombs, and the varying size and degree of workmanship of the associated stelae, all point to a strongly hierarchical aspect with regard to the relative status of the deceased entombed within the mortuary precincts.

DEDICATORY STONE THRONES AT AKSUM

Stone thrones, erected to commemorate a particular military campaign or some other major event, are believed to have been erected along the principal avenues leading to Aksum from the south and east. Some 25 such thrones were documented during the German Aksum Expedition (DAE) of 1906. Although dislodged from their *in situ* positions, they were found grouped into three clusters. Fifteen were located just west of the Church of Maryam Tseyon. The remaining 10 were located at the base of *Amba Mai Qoho*—five along a natural stone wall, and the remaining five just south of the latter.

WATER RESERVOIR AT AKSUM

At the base of the western slope of *Amba Mai Qoho*—within the central portion of the Mai Hejja Valley—a large reservoir impoundment for water had been constructed. The feature is called *Mai Shum*. It appears to have been the principal water supply for the entire residential population of Aksum for this period.

DISCUSSION

To begin with, the community of Aksum appears to have been laid out in a manner that suggests if not a plan, then at least a marked consideration for the orderly arrangement of functional precincts. Viewing the Mai Hejja Valley—lying between *Amba Bieta Giyorgis* and *Amba Mai Qoho*—as the principal northeast/southwest axis of the capital, one can see several key precincts. Positioned at the center of the valley is the Central Mortuary Precinct with its monumental stelae. At the northeast end of the valley is the *large town* of Adi

Quatia, where the majority of ordinary residents are believed to have resided. And at the southwest end is the *Eastern Palace Precinct*, where facilities for administration, the storage of export commodities, and the residential accommodations for the ruling elite and their retainers are believed to have been centered. Centrally positioned between the two residential precincts mentioned above was the water supply facility (the *Mai Shum*). The principal approaches to the Capital appear to have been from the west and east. As such, they would have passed the two flanking stelae fields—Gudit and Eastern—and approached the capital through the *Eastern Palace Precinct*, on avenues lined with dedicatory stone thrones.

The effect upon any visitor would have been enormous. The sheer scale of *palace* architecture, monumental thrones, and mortuary stelae, not to mention the dense concentration of an estimated 8,000 residents, would elicit a feeling of awe at the vision of such power and prestige. And should the visitor have any doubts, the graphic narratives of successful military conquests on the dedicatory stone thrones were there to offer verification. It would seem that the kingdom, in establishing its capital, sought to represent itself as the apex of political authority, ceremonial and religious ritual, and cosmopolitan living.

The most obvious political effect of the establishment of such a capital was to diminish the relative prestige and power of the local chiefdoms that are believed to have supplied the original military and political support for the kingdom during its *Early Phase*. Given the dramatic influx of new residents, and the scale of the many *palaces*, it is likely that many of the elite families that had previously resided elsewhere in the Aksumite realm sought residential proximity to the court, if not administrative positions. And those members of the elite that continued to reside within chiefly residential complexes elsewhere seem to have sought proximity in death—through entombment within one or another of the mortuary precincts that were concentrated at or near the capital.

One can well imagine that the *Late Phase* of the Early Aksumite Period was one in which the royal court—a collection of persons closely related or connected to the king and his extended family—gradually replaced the confederacy of local chiefdoms as the source of power and influence within the kingdom. They would appear to have accomplished this by magnifying the singular prestige of the king, and thereby distancing him from other elite lineages within the realm. But given the strong hierarchical dynamic implicit in mortuary arrangements, it would seem that even in the *Late Phase* there was sufficient credibility to the belief that all of the elite within the kingdom had some *relative* standing within the power structure of the realm. Certainly, many families invested heavily in tomb excavation, burial furnishings, and monolith extraction, transport, and erection, to validate their claim to a role in the governance of the kingdom.

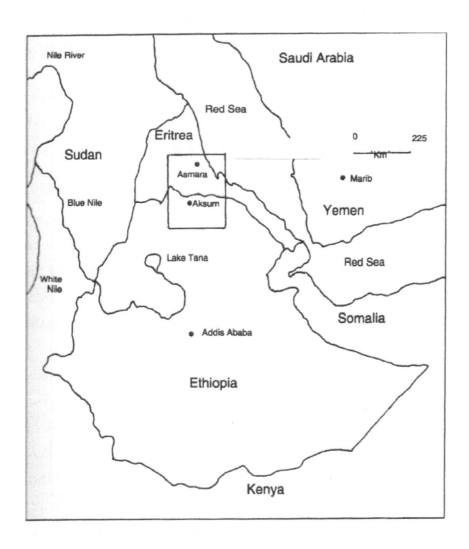

Figure 1—Aksumite Archaeological Zone in NE Africa

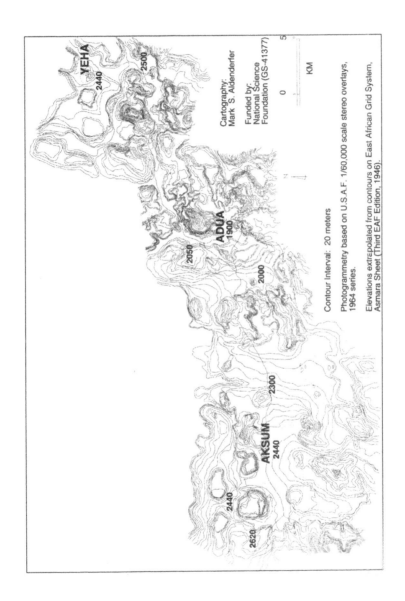

Figure 2—Segment of Shirè Plateau in which the Archaeological Survey was conducted

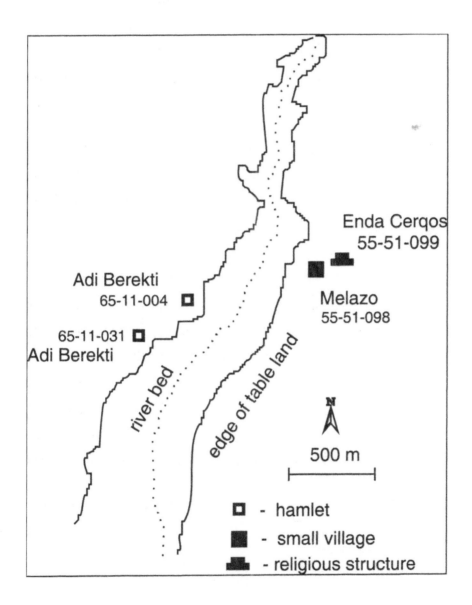

Figure 3—Mai Agazen Basin, Early Pre-Aksumite Period

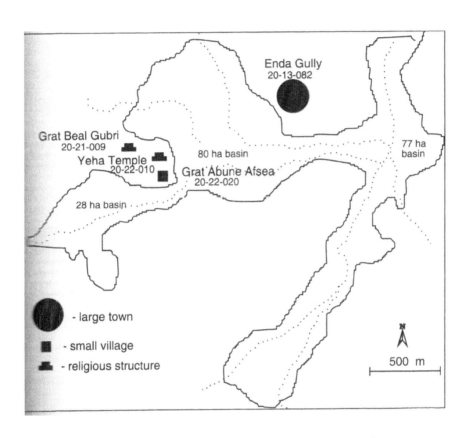

Figure 4—The Valley of Yeha: Early Pre-Aksumite Period

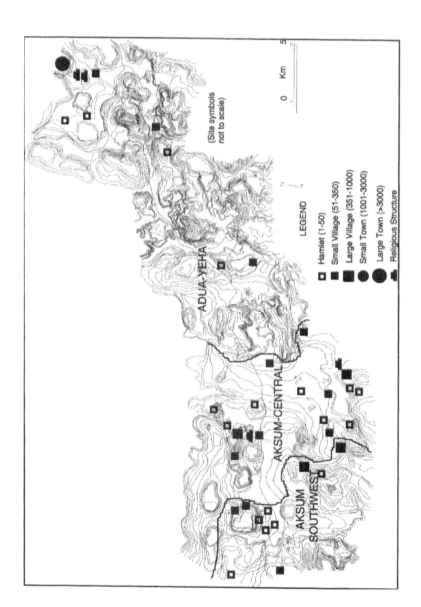

Figure 5—Subregional Settlement Groups, Early Pre-Aksumite Period

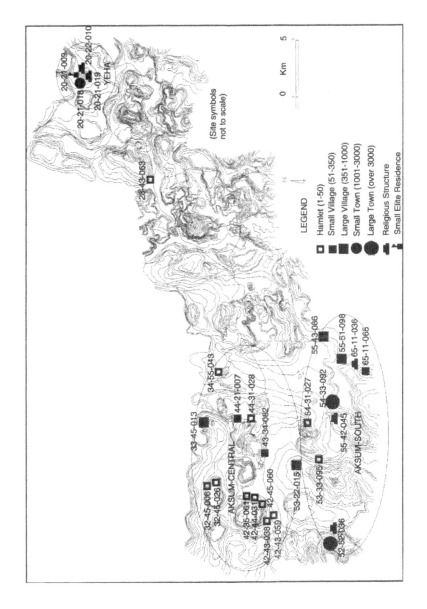

Figure 6—Middle Pre-Aksumite Settlement and Principal Sub-Regional Boundaries

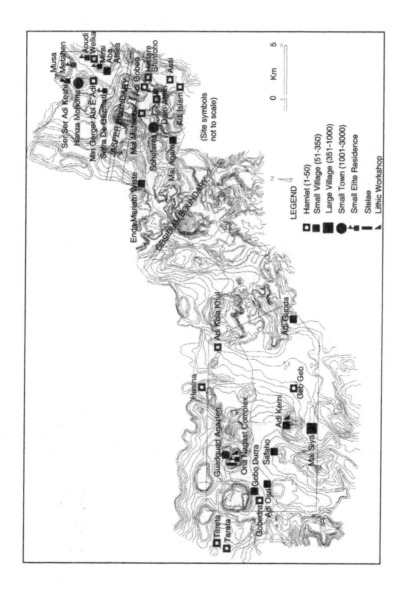

Figure 7—Late Pre-Aksumite Settlement: Subregional Interaction Spheres

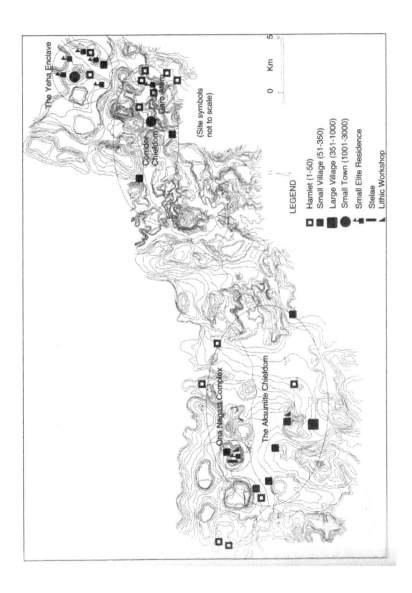

Figure 8—Late Pre-Aksumite Settlement: Regional Political Organization

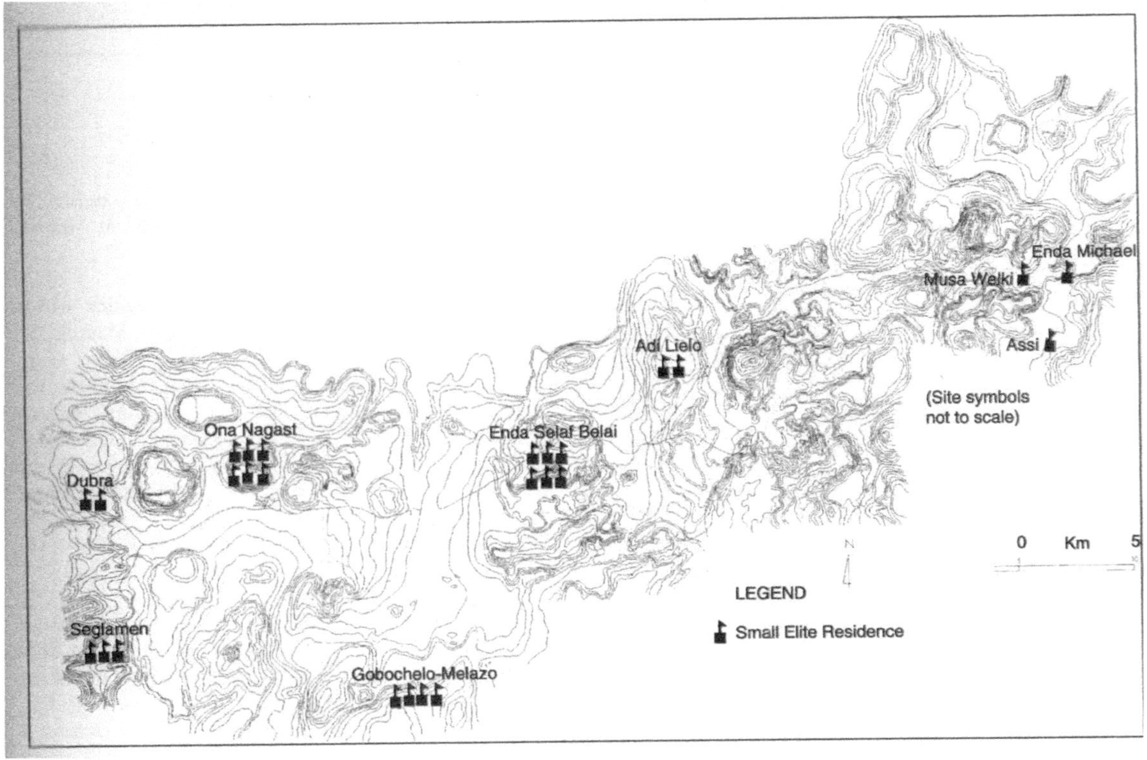

Figure 9—Early Aksumite Elite Residential Structures

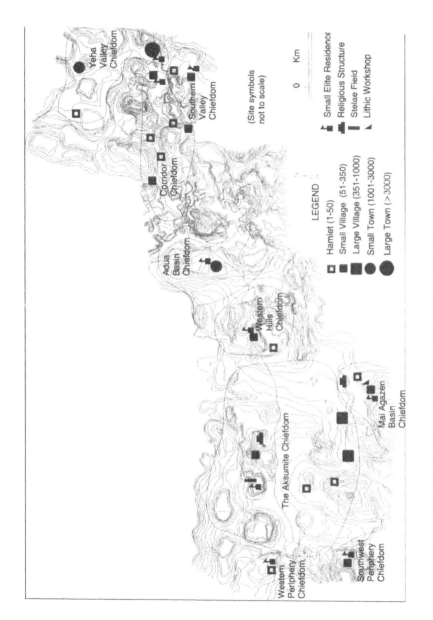

Figure 10—Early Aksumite Period: Early Phase Proliferation of Local Chiefdoms

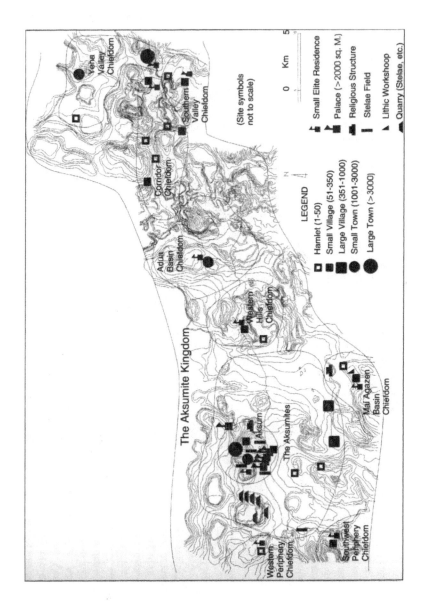

Figure 11—Early Aksumite Period: Late Phase Establishment of the Aksumite Capital

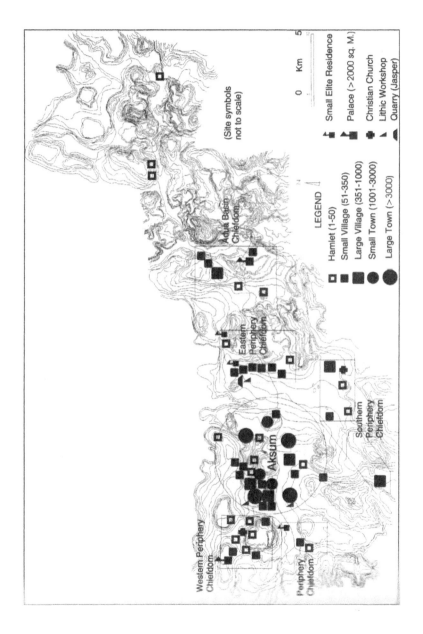

Figure 12—Late Aksumite Settlement: Metropolitan Aksum and Peripheral Local Chiefdoms

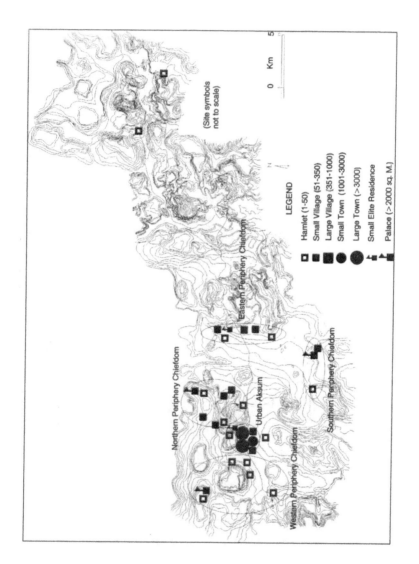

Figure 13—Early Post-Aksumite Settlement: Regional Political Organization

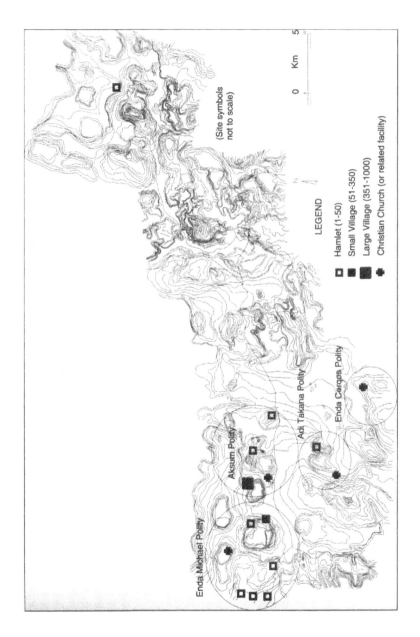

Figure 14—Late Post-Aksumite Settlement: Regional Political Organization

CHAPTER FIVE
The Late Aksumite Period

INTRODUCTION

The process that brought about the formation of a *state* level of political integration within the Aksumite Kingdom certainly dates back to the Late Pre-Aksumite Period when the chiefdom located on *Amba Bieta Giyorgis* that is identified with the *Ona Nagast Complex* (see Chapter 3) engaged in trade relations with kingdoms along the Nile River—from Upper Nubia to Egypt. The extraordinary concentration of wealth, local prestige, and administrative experience resulting from such contact clearly established that chiefdom on a trajectory of regional leadership and dominance.

Archaeological evidence presented in the previous chapter supports the notion that the Aksumites had succeeded in forming a robust interregional *kingdom* during the Early Aksumite Period. Many of the organizational elements of a *state* were put in place during that long era. But the remarkable transformation of the regional settlement pattern during the Late Aksumite Period, particularly as it affected the capital of Aksum, would seem to suggest that the *full* emergence of the *state* did not occur until then.

We shall observe that Aksum, the capital of the kingdom, becomes a metropolitan urban center of extraordinary proportions, that the layout of the capital appears to explicitly segregate and thereby highlight four principal *elite* institutions: (1) the royal palace, (2) the Christian cathedral and its leadership cadre, (3) the ruling elite and their constituent administrative complex, and (4) other resident elite of lesser proximity to the center of power. We shall also observe a profound shift in mortuary patterns that further enhances the singularity of status granted to the most highly ranking of the elite, while nullifying the pretensions of lesser elite. A full discussion of these and other developments are intended to illustrate the central point that the Aksumite Kingdom underwent significant political changes during the Late Aksumite Period—changes that this author believes led to the full emergence of a *state-level* political infrastructure.

SETTLEMENT PATTERN SUMMARY

Some 102 discrete archaeological entities are believed to date to the Late Aksumite Period. They are described in detail in the unabridged version of the book. The density of sites in and around Aksum was so great that several site distribution maps had to be prepared to fully accommodate the different categories of sites: residential communities of varying size, factory-scale workshops, quarries, palaces, elite residential structures, Christian churches, mortuary monuments, as well as cruciform shaft tombs.

Not all 102 discrete archaeological entities were residential in nature. The 84 that were residential, however, included 15 palaces, 12 elite residential structures, 20 hamlets 23 small villages, 6 large villages, 3 small towns, and 4 large towns. In total, it is estimated that the sampled portion of the region held about 42,000 people.

METROPOLITAN AKSUM

Metropolitan Aksum can be conceived of as a circle, 10 kilometers in diameter, centered roughly on *Amba Mai Qoho* that encloses an area of about 79 sq. kilometers. Within that circle are 60 archaeological entities: 5 *hamlets,* 9 *small villages,* 3 *large villages,* 3 *small towns,* 4 *large towns,* 9 *elite residences,* 14 *palaces,* 1 *cathedral,* 2 *factory-scale workshops,* and 10 *monumental or cruciform shaft tombs.*

The inventory is far from complete, since it only includes sites that have been documented. Approximately 39 sq. kilometers of area within Metropolitan Aksum has yet to be systematically surveyed and, given the somewhat serendipitous aspect to the discovery of cruciform shaft tombs in the Azi Kaleb precinct, it is likely that a number of both surface and subsurface archaeological entities dating to this period will be discovered in the years ahead.

THE URBAN POPULATION

Nevertheless, the site inventory we currently possess is sufficient to gain an appreciation for the extraordinary character of the Aksumite capital during this period. To begin with, the estimated population of Metropolitan Aksum is about 40,000, of which about 4,000 are believed to reside in elite residential settings, while about 36,000 are associated with non-elite residential settings. As such, Metropolitan Aksum comprises 90% of both the elite and non-elite population of the entire survey region during this period.

Quite clearly, the regional population has been drawn into the capital on an unprecedented scale. Whole portions of the region have been left with virtually no inhabitants: The Yeha Valley contains only a small Christian monastic order, the lands south of the Yeha Valley are without any settlements, and the Adua-Yeha Corridor contains only three modest *hamlets*. Thus, the population of three Early Aksumite Period local chiefdoms (presumably together with their leadership) appears to have been drawn within the capital: the *Yeha Valley Chiefdom*, the *Southern Valley Chiefdom*, and the *Corridor Chiefdom*.

Furthermore, the *Aksumites*, themselves, appear to have been drawn into the metropolitan precinct. Virtually the entire rural population of the Plain of Aksum is believed to have been drawn in, leaving the outlying portions of the fertile plain accessible to local chiefdoms drawn opportunistically to the periphery of the Plain from adjacent lands of less agricultural value.

And despite the presence of numerous smaller communities within the metropolitan precinct, a significant fraction of the population has coalesced into one or another of 10 large communities: 3 *large villages,* 3 *small towns*, and 4 *large towns*. Together, they represent the residential setting of about 34,000 inhabitants – some 86% of the population of Metropolitan Aksum.

But the absorption of even a significant fraction of the regional population by Metropolitan Aksum cannot account for its total size, since the population of the capital is now more than double what the entire regional population is estimated to have been during the Early Aksumite Period (40,000 vs 19,000). An analysis of ceramic variables given below is intended to shed light on the composition of Aksum's urban population, and to suggest some working hypotheses as to the possible origins of the constituent groups that make up that extraordinary metropolitan center.

CERAMIC ATTRIBUTE ANALYSIS

As one would expect, with the concentration of regional population within a fairly circumscribed area of the Aksumite Plateau, there is substantial similarity with respect to the decorative treatment and lip morphology of ceramic vessels among communities dating to the Late Aksumite Period. Still, the extraordinary increase in regional population, and the evidence provided by settlement pattern data that whole communities may have relocated, prompted this author to examine the ceramic attribute data carefully in the expectation that perhaps some subtle differences might emerge that would prove useful in understanding the composition of Metropolitan Aksum.

As it turned out, a selective focus upon a limited number of attribute classes within vessel lip morphology, and upon a single attribute class within the decorative treatment of vessel body sherds, has permitted the very tentative identification of four groups of non-elite residential settlements within Metropolitan Aksum.

GROUP #1

Group #1 is defined ceramically in terms of three progressively more exclusive characteristics. Its least exclusive characteristic—one shared with Groups #2 and #3 as well—is the percentage of rim sherds that fall within attribute categories LF-*unmodified*. The percentage ranges between 42% and 69%, leaving a substantial percentage of rim sherds remaining that were found to be more elaborately shaped (i.e. *bolstered, thickened, wedged, flanged,* etc.). The second characteristic is that the group—collectively—exhibits a *ratio* of 1:9 with respect to the frequency of rim sherds modified by *thickening* versus those involving the creation of a *wedge*. Group #2 shares the characteristic of significantly higher frequencies of *wedge-modified rims* relative to rims modified by *thickening* with

Group #1. Finally, and most exclusively, Group #1 is the only group of settlements within Metropolitan Aksum whose ceramic collections contained sherds characterized by a decorative treatment involving *incising (DT-shallow, narrow, simple linear (DT 16) or DT-complex linear (DT 30))*.

Group #1 consists of 12 settlements, ranging from *large towns* to *hamlets* that are estimated to have accommodated about 26,000 people—some 72% of the non-elite population within Metropolitan Aksum. The large communities that are in the immediate vicinity of the *Western Palace Precinct*, with its tight cluster of elite complexes, are all members of Group #1, as are the two largest *towns* within Metropolitan Aksum. It seems most likely that Group #1 represents the core population of the capital—being comprised of *Aksumites* from both the Early Aksumite Period capital as well as those from rural settings that had previously been scattered across the Aksumite Plateau.

GROUP #2

Group #2 consists of sites that share two ceramic indicators with Group #1: (1) the percentage of rim sherds that fall within LF-*unmodified*, and (2) the *ratio* of rims modified by *thickening* versus those involving the creation of a *wedge*. Group #2 differs from Group #1 in that none of the collections contained sherds that exhibited DT 16 or DT 30 decorative treatments. There is a very close resemblance between Group #2, as defined above, and one of the local chiefdoms that occupied the periphery of the

Aksumite Plain: the *Southern Periphery Chiefdom* (see Figure 12). Not only do the sites that comprise that chiefdom exhibit a comparably low percentage of rim sherds that fall within LF-*unmodified* (when computed for the aggregate of sites [55%]), and a comparably high ratio of *wedge rims* to *thickened rims*, but there is also a shared absence of sherds exhibiting DT 16 or DT 30 decorative treatments.

Group #2 contains only three settlements—all *small villages*—that comprise an estimated population of about 300 people. They are widely scattered, although in all cases they are located in the southern half of Metropolitan Aksum. Given the taxonomic resemblance between Group #2 and the *Southern Periphery Chiefdom*, and the modest number of settlements and respective residents involved, it is this author's opinion that the settlements of Group #2 have their origin within the population that previously occupied the *Southern Drainage* Physiographic Zone of the Aksumite Plateau.

GROUP #3

Group #3 shares with Groups #1 and #2 the characteristic of having 50% - 65% of rim sherds fall within attribute categories LF-*unmodified*. It differs from those Groups with respect to the *ratio* of sherds with *thickened rims* to those with *wedge-shaped* rims. In Groups #1 and #2 the *ratio* was 1:9 or greater, whereas in Group #3 the *ratio* is 1:2 (*thickened rims* to *wedge-shaped rims*). In both of these characteristics Group #3 strongly resembles settlements belonging to the *Eastern Periphery Chiefdom* and the *Adua Basin Chiefdom* (see Figure 12).

Although Group #3 only contains two settlements—one *small village* and one *hamlet*—involving an estimated total population of about 400, it does have the special distinction of having an *elite residential structure* (with an additional 90 or so inhabitants) associated with one of the settlements. The resemblance between Group #3 and chiefdoms located on the eastern edge of the Aksumite Plain or down in the Adua Basin suggests that the origin of the population most likely lies east of the Aksumite Plateau. A strikingly close resemblance also exists between Group #3 and the three remaining *hamlets* in the Adua-Yeha Corridor. Given the population deficit in that area, one can easily imagine that Group #3, with its elite residence, represents a relocated portion of the *Corridor Chiefdom* of the Early Aksumite Period (see Figures 10, 11).

GROUP #4

Group #4 is defined ceramically by two characteristics that appear to set it off from Groups #1, #2, and #3: (1) a high percentage of rim sherds that fall within the LF-*unmodified* category (75% - 100%), and (2) the virtual absence of rim sherds that fall within the LF-*thickened rims* category. Both characteristics are especially noteworthy since three of the sites yielded very large sherd collections (n=1200).

In fact, the pottery vessels associated with the sites in this group exhibited remarkably little decorative treatment of any sort. Two sites had only 4 body sherds with decorative treatment, and one site had only 11 such sherds. This is all the more surprising due to the proximity of these sites to some of the larger Group #1 sites in Metropolitan Aksum that exhibited substantial decorative treatment of pottery vessels.

Group #4 consists of six sites: 1 *large town,* 1 *small town,* 2 *large villages*, 1 *small village*, and 1 *hamlet*. Together, they represent an estimated population of about 8000—23% of the non-elite population of the capital. Over half that total (about 4600 persons) reside within a single *large town* that is directly associated with a *palace* site that is estimated to have accommodated another 140 or so persons. The sites are widely distributed within Metropolitan Aksum, and do not constitute an *enclave* of any sort.

Not only does Group #4 not resemble any of the other groups in Metropolitan Aksum, it also does not resemble any of the local chiefdoms distributed elsewhere within the survey region. Nevertheless, one is tempted to view Group #4 as the relocated *Yeha Valley Chiefdom* of the Early Aksumite Period. That political entity had an estimated population of about 5000 (both elite & non-elite), which compares nicely with the estimated 4800 (elite & non-elite) of the Group #4 complex. But with no way to test that hypothesis, it remains entirely speculative.

One of the drawbacks to the above hypothesis is the lack of decorative elaboration of the ceramic assemblage that constitutes a key diagnostic of Group #4. One would imagine that a relocated Yeha Valley Chiefdom population would display more elaborate decorative treatment and greater diversity of vessel lip morphology—analogous to what is encountered among the ceramic assemblages of all the other sites within the survey region. From this standpoint, there is a better chance that the relocated *Yeha Valley Chiefdom*—should it be within Metropolitan Aksum—is to be found among one or more of the Group #1 settlements.

This leaves us with a default hypothesis, namely that the settlements of Group #4 represent communities that have been relocated to Metropolitan Aksum from *outside* the Aksum-Yeha Survey Region. But this also presents a problem, for the fact that seriation analysis was able to successfully assign the *ceramic ware* profiles of the sites in Group #4 to the Late Aksumite matrix homostat argues strongly for strong geographic proximity.

Thus the most prudent explanation for Group #4 would seem to be that it represents communities that lie either at the farthest reaches of the survey region—such as the Yeha Valley area—or areas outside but immediately adjacent to the survey region—perhaps as far as Selak Laka to the west, or Adigrat to the east. In either case, we appear to be dealing with a decidedly rural population, given the simplicity of its ceramic micro-tradition.

One can thus conclude that during the Late Aksumite Period Metropolitan Aksum had become a highly urbanized capital whose resident non-elite population was comprised not only of members of the *Aksumite Chiefdom*, and those of other local chiefdoms within the survey region, but perhaps also by immigrant communities from outside the survey area. Compared to the Early Aksumite Period capital (est. pop. 8,000), Metropolitan Aksum is dramatically larger (by more than 300%), more densely urban, and most likely more ethnically diverse.

THE URBAN ELITE

There has been an explosive growth in the number of elite residential settings within the capital between the *Late Phase* of the Early Aksumite Period and the period under discussion—from a total of 6 *palaces* to an aggregate of 23 elite complexes (14 *palaces* and 9 *elite residential structures*). Despite the 280% increase in elite residential settings, there was only a doubling of the estimated number of residents occupying those facilities (from about 2000 to about 4000).

Quite obviously, only some undetermined fraction of those residents were themselves members of the elite. These would have included the principal extended family for whom the resident complex had been constructed, together with other members of the elite who served in responsible administrative roles within the complex. The remaining residents would have been non-elite retainers of one category or another.

However, the two indices—number of residential settings and number of estimated residents—can be usefully viewed as reflecting two different aspects of the urban elite. The first indicator—number of elite residential settings—probably measures the actual growth in the size of the elite population within the capital as well as can be expected within an archaeological database. From this standpoint, one can argue that the elite population of the capital grew by 280% between the *Late Phase* of the Early Aksumite Period and the Late Aksumite Period.

The second indicator—number of estimated residents within elite settings—can be viewed as measuring the size of the administrative infrastructure within the capital. The architectural layout of *elite residential complexes*, regardless of size, supports the notion that they were built to accommodate a variety of functions, including those one would deem *administrative*. The elite residential settings were, among other things, the *office complexes* of the capital. Using this measure, one can argue that the administrative infrastructure of the capital of Aksum grew by 100% between the *Late Phase* of the Early Aksumite Period and the Late Aksumite Period.

THE LAYOUT OF METROPOLITAN AKSUM

In the preceding chapter, it was observed that during the *Late Phase* of the Early Aksumite Period the capital of Aksum appeared to have been laid out in a manner that gave consideration to the orderly arrangement of functional precincts. The Central Mortuary District, with its monumental stelae, served as the geographic and symbolic center of the capital. To the north were the large urban communities within which the majority of ordinary residents are believed to have resided. And to the south, a cluster of *palaces* formed what appears to have been the paramount elite and administrative precinct. The principal approaches to the capital—from the east and west—passed flanking stelae fields and entered the capital along avenues lined with monumental dedicatory stone thrones.

In the Late Aksumite Period, there has been both continuity and change. Fundamentally, the layout of Metropolitan Aksum highlights four principal political institutions: the *Royal Palace*, the *Christian Church*, the *Ruling Elite*, and the *Resident Elite*.

In the Early Aksumite Period there was no discernible spatial distinction between the *palaces* of the *Ruling Elite* and that of the *king*. All five *palaces* documented south of the Central Mortuary District formed a loose cluster in what this author refers to as the *Eastern Palace Precinct*, located east of the Mai Lahlaha stream bed, west of the Mai Hejja stream bed, and north of the Gondar/Adua Highway.

However, this changes dramatically in the Late Aksumite Period. Only a single *palace*—Taakha Maryam—can be documented within the *Eastern Palace Precinct* at this time. The *Eastern Palace Precinct* may thus have become an even more exclusive section of the capital—dedicated perhaps to the residency of the king (assuming the newly constructed *palace* of Taakha Maryam was the royal residence). Kobischanov (1979:97) suggests just that in his assertion that the central structure of the Taakha Maryam architectural complex was the *palace* described by Cosmas Indicopleustes in his reference to the *"four-turreted palace of the king of Ethiopia"*(Winstedt 1899).

In contrast, west of the Mai Lahlaha stream bed, and bordering upon the Gondar/Adua Highway, in a neighborhood referred to locally as *Daro Addi Kilte,* one encounters a very dense cluster of 12 elite residential complexes, consisting of 6 *palaces* and 6 *elite residential structures.* In most cases, the outer walls of adjacent complexes are separated from each other by only relatively short intervals of open space. One may refer to this as the *Western Palace Precinct.* This appears to be the administrative center of the capital—where the *Ruling Elite* resided, and where most of the administrative functions of government were carried out.

The Mai Lahlaha stream bed forms a clear geographic partition between the two palace precincts, and thus tends to segregate the tight cluster of elite complexes from the singular setting of the Taakha Maryam *palace*. One cannot help but speculate that this spatial distinction reflects a political transformation involving the clear separation of the office of the King from that of the offices of the administrative bureaucracy.

The monumental edifice of Maryam Tseyon, the Christian Cathedral of Aksum, was located about 500 meters northeast of the *palace* of Taakha Maryam. An Annex to the cathedral involving what appears to have been a *palace-scale* elite residential and administrative complex (Enda Maryam) was located just 20 meters north of the outer wall of the cathedral grounds.

Although Christianity appears to have had a presence in the kingdom since the 4th Century AD, it was not until the Late Aksumite Period that it fully evolved into an institutionalized state religion. As such, it performed a key support role in the governance of the kingdom. Small, outlying churches in rural areas of the survey region begin to be observed in the archaeological record. And in the ruined shell of the Temple of Yeha a small church and resident monastic community (Beta Christian) is believed to have been established at this time. With its governmentally sanctioned prominence as the center of religious life within the kingdom, its monumental cathedral, and its rural network of churches and monastic communities, Christianity constituted a powerful but separate arm of the state.

The spatial separation of the church complex from both the *Eastern* and *Western Palace Precincts* reinforces the impression that the governing infrastructure had become both more complex and more formally institutionalized—with each institution having well-defined lines of responsibility and the support of proprietary administrative cadres.

North of the Mai Hejja Valley (that lies between *Amba Bieta Giyorgis* and *Amba Mai Qoho*), and extending in a wide arc almost as far as the plateau escarpment, one encounters a loose cluster of elite complexes, consisting of 6 *palaces* and 3 *elite residential structures* that form part of Metropolitan Aksum. Unlike the elite complexes in the *Palace Precincts* to the south, 5 of the 9 elite complexes in this *Northern Cluster* are directly associated with non-elite residential settlements. That fact, together with the fact that the *Northern Cluster* is separated by the physical barriers of the *ambas,* and by the intervening presence of a *small town* directly within the Mai Hejja Valley, suggests that the *Resident Elite* of the *Northern Cluster* probably represent the leadership of communities who are removed somewhat from the center of power. They are being referred to as the *Resident Elite* in contrast to the *Ruling Elite* (i.e. those who occupy the *Western Palace Precinct).*

The *Resident Elite* are believed to form a fourth distinct institutional arm of the Aksumite State. Based upon the ceramic analysis given in an earlier section of this chapter, the elite complexes of the *Northern Cluster* include leadership affiliated with Group #1 settlements (*Core Aksumites),* Group #3 settlements (relocated from the Adua-Yeha Corridor, most likely), and Group #4 settlements (*Immigrants* from *Outside the Survey Region or from its periphery*). The presence of elites relocated from elsewhere within the survey region or from outside the region supports the idea that the Late Aksumite Period witnessed an increase in the centralization of political authority—a characteristic of emergent states.

ELITE MORTUARY PATTERNS

There appears to have been a profound shift in elite mortuary patterns with the onset of the Late Aksumite Period. To begin with, the practice of erecting stelae to mark the location of subterranean tombs comes to an end. Furthermore, with a few exceptions, the mortuary precincts associated with the principal stelae fields—*Central, Gudit, Bieta Giyorgis, Eastern*, and *Medoque*—appear no longer to have served as a locus for interment. The adoption of Christianity may have played some role in bringing the era of stelae markers to an end, but the fact that a decidedly Christian structure such as the *Tomb of the False Door* (Munro-Hay 1989:152) was installed in the Central Mortuary District of Aksum suggests that the subsequent abandonment of these elite burial grounds cannot be attributed exclusively to the influences of Christianity.

Although Munro-Hay (*ibid*) makes the point that the stelae seem to have been left intact after their abandonment, not having incurred any mutilation as a consequence of ideological zealousness, the same cannot be said for the stelae fields themselves. In at least two cases—the Bieta Giyorgis Stelae Field and the Central Mortuary District of Aksum—archeological evidence indicates that non-elite settlements were installed directly among the stelae, blanketing the entirety of both mortuary precincts.

In the case of Bieta Giyorgis, a *large village* of Late Aksumite date overlies the burial/ceremonial precinct. In the case of the Central Mortuary District, which covers an area of 7 hectares, it is estimated that a *small town* of Late Aksumite Period date overlies the district, providing residential accommodations for over a thousand people.

The two instances cited above inevitably suggest that the societal role of the Early Aksumite Period stelae fields had come to an end with the onset of the Late Aksumite Period. More intriguing, perhaps, is the fact that the *large village* overlying the Bieta Giyorgis Stelae Field is a Group #4 community based upon ceramic attribute analysis, and thereby believed to represent an *immigrant settlement*. Since we have no ceramic data, one can only speculate as to whether the same is true of the *small town* (Haoulti) that covers the Central Mortuary District. In the case of such a *Guest Settlement*, one would imagine that explicit permission of the king would need to have been secured with respect to community location. Royal acquiescence in the positioning of non-elite settlements directly on top of the elite mortuary precincts of the Early Aksumite Era kingdom requires a political explanation.

That explanation will need to take into account the mortuary practices of the elite that characterized the Late Aksumite Period, and which therefore reflected the subsequent sociopolitical role of elite mortuary behavior within Metropolitan Aksum.

Elite mortuary sites documented so far for the Late Aksumite Period appear to represent two contrasting forms. One form is what Munro-Hay refers to as the *house/church memorial* (*ibid*), exemplified by the *Tombs of Kaleb and Gabra Masqal*. The other is the *cruciform shaft tomb*, which can accommodate multiple interments. Both types of tombs appear to be concentrated in the area north of the Mai Hejja Valley—particularly in the Azi Kaleb and Adi Watot districts.

The predominantly Christian symbolic themes, such as the cruciform shape of the shaft tombs, and the carved cross on a sarcophagus in the *Tomb of Gabra Masqal* suggest that the Azi Kaleb area took over as the principal mortuary precinct of the capital during the Christian dominated era of the Late Aksumite Period. Future archaeological investigation will in all likelihood reveal that the Azi Kaleb area contains many more *cruciform shaft tombs* that date to this period.

Two issues present themselves as we consider the political significance of these changes in elite mortuary practices: first, the location of the new mortuary district, and second, the implications of having two contrasting forms of mortuary sites.

The fact that a new location was deemed desirable suggests that the authorities sought to disassociate both royal and elite interments of the new era from those of the past. Some sort of clean break with the past was sought, and although a part of the rationale may have been religious the fact that Christian interments occurred within the Central Mortuary District argues for a more comprehensive explanation. A key feature of the stelae fields was that *all* members of the elite, regardless of rank, conceivably had the opportunity to secure burial in one or another of the cemeteries, and to erect a stele in commemoration—albeit the size of the monolith and the extent of masonry dressing would vary. Thus the stelae fields provided a dramatic testament to an earlier era of the kingdom, a time when the leadership of local chiefdoms—both within and outside the survey region—could claim some role in governance, however minor. One can well imagine that the emergent state, with its strong monarchical institution and its centralization of power, would wish to disassociate itself from that earlier era.

The adoption of two contrasting forms of interment sites could be viewed as a device to ensure that the politically important distinction between the *nobility [elite]* and the *most highly ranked elite [members of the royal family, e.g.]* was exemplified in mortuary behavior. Using the *Tombs of Kaleb and Gabra Masqal* as an example, one could argue that the *house/church memorial* tomb form represents the form intended for the interment of the most highly ranked members of the elite. In such cases, the subterranean tomb is marked by the presence of a monumental masonry superstructure that is conspicuous on the landscape. In contrast, the *cruciform shaft tomb* is simply a subterranean repository for the remains of multiple members of an elite extended family without a superstructure that would call undo attention to itself.

The new location of the elite mortuary district is itself an object worthy of attention. Located in the northern quadrant of Metropolitan Aksum, in an area far removed from the center of power, and one without any past mortuary tradition, one cannot but imagine that the role of the mortuary monument as a status marker of sociopolitical significance has been diminished. This would be understandable in the capital of a state-level society where *achieved status* competed with *ascribed status* as a basis for political participation.

PERIPHERAL LOCAL CHIEFDOMS

Surrounding Metropolitan Aksum, one can observe five local chiefdoms (see Figure 12). There appears to be a measure of continuity between these five chiefdoms and those of the Early Aksumite Period that occupied the periphery of the Aksumite Plateau and the Adua Basin area. It has already been noted that the three Early Aksumite chiefdoms located in the Yeha Valley and Adua-Yeha Corridor areas (see Figures 10, 11) are believed to have been relocated to Metropolitan Aksum. Why a similar fate did not befall those chiefdoms in closer proximity to the capital remains a question. But two possible explanations seem worth consideration: (1) access to the fertile soils of the Plain of Aksum, and (2) the importance of key highway junctions east and west of the capital. How these two factors might have affected local chiefdoms will be explored in the discussions that follow.

The more fundamental question is what political role, if any, did these local chiefdoms play in a kingdom that appears now to have achieved full *state* status? To begin with, it appears that the local chiefdoms of the Early Aksumite Period did not disappear with the full transformation of the kingdom into a *state*. As we observed in the discussion of Metropolitan Aksum, there is some reason to believe that even after a presumed relocation to the capital elements of both the *Corridor Chiefdom* and the *Yeha Chiefdom* are still recognizable.

The most economical explanation is that their role in governance was diminished as an accretion of new layers of governmental elite were interposed between the leadership of the local chiefdoms and the office of the king. But the economic role of such local chiefdoms would have continued to be important, and for that reason, most likely, they survived remarkably intact. One can imagine that local chiefs organized agricultural activity within rural areas at the periphery of the metropolitan area, yet close enough to contribute to the domestic economy of the capital. Even the local chiefdoms believed to have relocated to Metropolitan Aksum from the Adua-Yeha Corridor and the Yeha Valley may have continued to organize agricultural activity.

They would have been positioned to supervise agricultural activity in the northeast quadrant of the metropolitan area—an area particularly productive agriculturally owing to the presence of highly fertile soils. A discussion of each of the five local chiefdoms identified in Figure 12 follows.

THE EASTERN PERIPHERY CHIEFDOM

The *Eastern Periphery Chiefdom*, so named because the communities that make up the chiefdom are located on the eastern periphery of the Plain of Aksum, consists of 6 *small villages*, 2 *hamlets*, and 2 *elite residential structures* (see Figure 12). The chiefdom is believed to be a Late Aksumite Period manifestation of the *Western Hills Chiefdom* of the Early Aksumite Period (see Figures 10, 11). Two of the sites within the *Eastern Periphery Chiefdom* continue to be located just east of the interface between the Aksumite Plain and the Western Hills section of the Adua Basin. The working hypothesis is that as the settlements of rural farmers of the Aksumite Plain were drawn into urban concentrations within Metropolitan Aksum, farming communities on the periphery of the Aksumite Plateau, such as those affiliated with the *Western Hills Chiefdom,* were encouraged to relocate their settlements and begin cultivating the superior soils at the edge of the Plain. In fact, Figure 11 suggests that the area newly colonized by the chiefdom had not actually been occupied during the previous period.

In addition to farming, however, residents of the *Eastern Periphery Chiefdom*, particularly those in the community of Enda Jesus, appear to have had a proprietary connection with the large jasper quarry of Adi Kushow located nearby, and to have engaged in factory-scale craft or processing operations at both the quarry and the village location.

Ceramic analysis reveals that the *Eastern Periphery Chiefdom* can be characterized by several features—two of which we have already encountered in our discussion of the site groupings in Metropolitan Aksum: (1) an average that falls between 50% - 65% of rim sherds (51%) within the LF-*unmodified* category, and (2) a *ratio* of *thickened rims* to *wedge* rims [when averaged] of 1:2. In addition, however, the cluster of sites believed to be affiliated with the chiefdom share in common decorative techniques: DT-*grooved* and DT-*punctate*.

THE WESTERN PERIPHERY CHIEFDOM

Anchored by the *Palace* at Bergerawi, the *Western Periphery Chiefdom* consists of 5 *hamlets,* 3 *small villages*, and a *Christian Church,* that occupy elevated land surfaces surrounding the Fil Filli Valley—an agriculturally favorable locale just to the west of Metropolitan Aksum. The chiefdom is believed to be a continuation of the *Western Periphery Chiefdom* of the Early Aksumite Period. As in the case of the *Eastern Periphery Chiefdom*, this one also appears to have capitalized on the apparent concentration of *Aksumite* farmers within Metropolitan Aksum—a legacy of the Early Aksumite Period—by shifting their communities from the less favorable setting at the western edge of the Aksumite Plateau into the unoccupied Fil Filli Valley.

Ceramic analysis reveals two contrasting features between the chiefdom under discussion and the *Eastern Periphery Chiefdom*. They both share the feature of having an average that falls between 50% - 65% of rim sherds (58%) within the LF-*unmodified* category, but vary with respect to the *ratio* of *thickened rims* to *wedge rims*. In the *Western Periphery Chiefdom* the *ratio* (averaged among all eight sites) is 1:6 (as opposed to a [averaged] *ratio* of 1:2). Secondly, they differ with respect to diagnostic decorative technique attributes: Eastern Periphery Chiefdom is characterized by *grooved* & *punctate* techniques, while the Western Periphery Chiefdom is characterized by the *fluted* technique.

THE SOUTHERN PERIPHERY CHIEFDOM

Unlike the two local chiefdoms already discussed, the *Southern Periphery* Chicfdom is not anchorcd by a *'known' elite residential complex*. The mounding east of the Mai Agazen Basin is fairly complex, and it is this author's opinion that such a residential complex dating to this period will eventually be found in that area. In its place, however, is the Christian Church of Enda Cerqos. The presence of the church documents the fact that the northern end of the Mai Agazen Basin constitutes a politically nuclear area—a legacy that the basin has enjoyed as far back as the Pre-Aksumite Era. In addition to the church, the chiefdom consists of 2 *large villages*, 1 *small village* and 2 *hamlets*, based upon present archaeological evidence (see Figure 12).

As in the case of the two local chiefdoms already discussed, the *Southern Periphery Chiefdom* is believed to be a continuation of an Early Aksumite Period chiefdom – in this case the *Mai Agazen Basin Chiefdom* (see Figures 10, 11). Similarly, there appears to have been a shift onto the highly fertile soils of the Aksumite Plain from the less desirable soils at the periphery of the Aksumite Plateau—in this case, from the Southern Drainage Physiographic Zone. However, not all communities believed to be part of the chiefdom made the shift. The *large village* of Gobo Debre, linked to the chiefdom on the basis of ceramic analysis, is positioned well within the *Southern Drainage* area.

The three ceramic indicators used to characterize local chiefdoms have the following values with respect to the *Southern Periphery Chiefdom*. The percentage of rim sherds that fall within the LF-*unmodified* category is (in aggregate) 55%. In this respect, it resembles the two chiefdoms already discussed. The *ratio* of *thickened rims* to *wedge rims,* however, sets it apart since [in aggregate] it exhibits a *ratio* of 1:15. It is further set apart from the others with respect to Decorative Technique. Those techniques that appear to be diagnostic for the *Southern Periphery Chiefdom* are *grooved* and *fillet.*

THE PERIPHERY CHIEFDOM

This is the most problematic of the local chiefdoms. An *elite residence structure* known as Gobo Durra, is located just west of Metropolitan Aksum, directly overlooking the present-day Gondor-Adua Highway. About 3 kilometers southwest of Gobo Durra, in the immediate vicinity of a principal road junction, one encounters a *small village* and a *hamlet* (see Figure 12). The three sites share some ceramic attribute characteristics. The percentage of rim sherds that fall within the LF-*unmodified* category approximates the 50% to 65% range observed among all of the other local chiefdoms. All three sites exhibit a *ratio* of *thickened rims* to *wedge rims* that is closer to the 1:2 *ratio* than to the 1:6 or higher *ratio*. And all three sites can be grouped together on the basis of a shared Decorative Technique attribute: DT-*grooved*. But the paucity of sites, and the distance separating the communities from the *elite residence complex*, pose questions as to the validity of grouping the three sites into a local chiefdom configuration.

The most compelling explanatory framework that this author can come up with to explain the spatial anomaly, should this group of sites represent a local chiefdom, is that the distribution of the sites is a byproduct of an ancient road junction. Both of the residential community sites within the group are located along the south fork of a road junction. The elite residence is on the main road between the junction and Metropolitan Aksum. If one hypothesized that other residential communities—not yet identified—were located along the north fork west of the junction then a coherent distribution pattern would obtain. Why a local chiefdom would find it particularly attractive to position itself along principal roads leading to Aksum is another question, and one for which this author has no answer. But the fact that the chiefdom to be discussed next—the *Adua Basin Chiefdom*—has precisely that distribution pattern enhances the probability that something of the sort may be operating with respect to this chiefdom.

Assuming this is a local chiefdom, the next question is where did it come from? The most obvious antecedent candidate is the *Southwest Periphery Chiefdom* of the Early Aksumite Period (see Figures 10, 11). From its earlier location at the extreme southwestern corner of the Survey Region, at the interface of the Southern Drainage Physiographic Zone and the Western Periphery Physiographic Zone, it would have a strong incentive to move north on to the Aksumite Plain. We have argued for comparable relocations with respect to all of the other periphery chiefdoms. Furthermore, the antecedent chiefdom may have already established a precedent of being associated with a principal highway, since it would appear that the south fork of the highway leading to Aksum continues southward right past the Early Aksumite Period location of the chiefdom. In this scenario, the population of the antecedent chiefdom simply followed the road northward, resettling in an area that provided access to the fertile soils of the Aksumite Plain but also to what appears to have been a key road junction just west of Metropolitan Aksum.

THE ADUA BASIN CHIEFDOM

The *Adua Basin Chiefdom* offers the clearest case of continuity between the chiefdoms of the Early Aksumite Period and those of the Late Aksumite Period (compare Figure 12 with Figures 10,11). The principal residential settlement of the Early Aksumite Period chiefdom—Adi Asao—continues to serve that role in the Late Aksumite Period. The chiefdom consists of 1 *large village,* 3 *small villages*, and 2 *hamlets*. The chiefly residence is identified as Adi Nasa—an *elite residential structure* associated with a *small village* of the same name.

The ceramic attribute characteristics of the group of sites identified with the chiefdom include the percentage of rim sherds that fall within LF-*unmodified* (it approximates the 50% - 65% range that appears to be characteristic of the other local chiefdoms and also of three of the four site groups within Metropolitan Aksum). And the *ratio* of LF-*thickened rims* to LF-*Wedge Rims* is 1:2—comparable to that of the *Eastern Periphery Chiefdom,* and of the Group #3 sites within Metropolitan Aksum. The diagnostic decorative technique attribute of the *Adua Basin Chiefdom* appears to be DT-*grooved*. This sets it apart from all other local chiefdoms except for the neighboring *Eastern Periphery Chiefdom*, where DT-*grooved* formed one of three diagnostic DT attributes.

Given the presumed Late Aksumite Period relocation to Metropolitan Aksum, or onto the Aksumite Plain, of the other Early Aksumite local chiefdoms within the Survey Region, the question arises as to why that pattern was not implemented with respect to the *Adua Basin Chiefdom*? The Adua Basin Physiographic Zone is characterized by soils inferior to those of the Aksumite Plain. And the Subregional Market System of the ethnographic present (1974) clearly suggests that settlements in the Adua Basin area did not fall within the market orbit of Aksum. This would suggest that the movement of domestic commodities, such as food, from the Adua Basin area to Metropolitan Aksum would have represented a non-optimal logistical arrangement.

An examination of the settlement pattern of the *Adua Basin Chiefdom* offers one possible explanation. Four of the residential sites within the chiefdom are aligned along the fork of the principal highway approaching Aksum from the northeast, while the chiefly residence and associated village of Adi Nasa occupies a position in the vicinity of the fork of that highway approaching Aksum from the southeast (see Figure 12). Together, the sites of the *Adua Basin Chiefdom* appear to envelope the two principal highways just east of the junction where they meet. If one assumes that the principal ancient roadways were positioned similarly, then one could argue that the logic of the settlement pattern is intelligible with reference to the highway pattern.

CHAPTER SIX
The Early Post-Aksumite Period

INTRODUCTION

The period beginning around the middle of the 8th Century AD, according to Kobischanov (1979:117), *"was characterized by a gradual weakening of royal authority, a decline of cities and trade, growing isolation, and progressive political fragmentation."* Aksum had ceased to be the capital of the kingdom (*ibid:120*), and the ruler of the kingdom was no longer called *King of Aksum*, but rather *Hadani* (*ibid*). According to written Ethiopian tradition (*ibid*), the Aksumite dynasty came to an end in 896 or 898 AD.

Thus the Early Post-Aksumite Period offers us a snapshot of the effects of the decline and eventual collapse of the Aksumite Kingdom upon the region under study. We shall observe that the four principal political institutions highlighted in the layout of Metropolitan Aksum during the Late Aksumite Period—the *Royal Palace*, the *Christian Church*, the *Ruling Elite*, and the *Resident Elite*—are no longer in evidence. Furthermore, we will note that the population of Metropolitan Aksum contracts by 77%, forming a tightly-clustered urban core that takes up residence among the ruins of the abandoned *Western Palace Precinct* and areas immediately adjacent to it. And the long tradition of elaborate mortuary patterns for the elite comes to an end. Finally, we no longer observe archaeological evidence for the presence of factory-scale workshops among the regional population, with the implication that long-distance trade had most likely ceased to be an important part of the regional economy.

In contrast, however, we shall observe that the peripheral chiefdoms of the Aksumite Plateau continue to flourish. But a sharp dichotomy between urban and rural populations with respect to ceramic micro-tradition suggests that the two worlds are politically and economically independent of one another. And the depopulation of subregions east of the Aksumite Plateau continues, with the disappearance of all traces of settlement in the Adua Basin area.

POLITICAL ANALYSIS

A total of 31 sites, involving 33 discrete archaeological entities, are believed to date to the Early Post-Aksumite Period. All 33 of the discrete archaeological entities were residential in nature.

AKSUM

Aksum consists of a group of 5 tightly clustered settlements within an area of less than 1 sq. kilometer (see Figure 13). The

5 sites—2 *large towns*, 1 *small town*, and 2 *small villages*—represent an urban population estimated to have been about 9000 people. Urban Aksum is centered on the complex of *palace* and *elite residence* ruins abandoned at the end of the Late Aksumite Period that constituted the *Western Palace Precinct* [and known in the present period as the *Daro Addi Kilte Residential Zone*]. The 1939 excavations by Salvatore Puglisi of the ruins popularly known as *"Puglisi's Villa"*—a component of the *Western Palace Precinct*—offer us a picture of that process: non-elite dwellings being erected against the walls of the partial ruins; forming what may have been an almost continuous expanse of *apartment-styled* living accommodations that utilized the multiple rooms of the elite structures and the intervening spaces between them.

About 300 meters northeast of the *Daro Addi Kilte Residential Zone*, and positioned on an overlooking terrace, was the *Elite Residential Structure* of Jana Duk. This is the only elite residence so far documented for Aksum in the Early Post-Aksumite Period. Its full dimensions are not yet known since only a small wall segment had been exposed, but it remains the most likely structure to have served as the residence of the political ruler of Aksum during the Early Post-Aksumite Period. The existence of such a political ruler is attested to in one of the inscriptions of Hadani Dan'el (DAE, IV, No. 14)(Kobishchanov 1979:120), which makes reference to a local ruler of Aksum—one who served as a vassal of the Hadani himself.

An analysis of ceramic attributes suggests that the population of urban Aksum possessed a distinctive ceramic micro-tradition that involved the shared presence of multiple decorative treatments. On average, 5.6% of all body sherds collected from an urban Aksum site exhibited decorative treatment. Seven different decorative treatments (DT) were to be found in each of the 7 ceramic sampling units associated with urban Aksum: an *incised* variant (DT16), 3 *grooved variants* (DT43, DT45, DT46), a *fluted variant* (DT47), a *ribbed* variant (DT49), and a *punctate* variant (DT57). *Ribbed* sherds were by far the most numerous, although sherds with *punctate* or the DT43 variant of *grooved* treatment were also numerous. In summary, one can conclude that urban Aksum possessed a rich variety of decorative treatments within its ceramic assemblage. Most noteworthy, however, is the fact that such diversity was significantly less common in the ceramic assemblages of the surrounding local chiefdoms.

LOCAL CHIEFDOMS

Rural settlement within the survey region during this period was almost entirely confined to the Aksumite Plateau (see Figure 13). Two *hamlets* were documented east of the plateau—one within the Adua-Yeha Corridor and the other in the hill and valley system south of the Yeha Valley. But the *Adua Basin Chiefdom*, so prominent in the Late Aksumite Period, has completely disappeared. On the Aksumite Plateau, however, there are 13 *hamlets* and 8 *small villages* that comprise a rural population estimated at about 1900 people when the residents of the 4 elite structures associated with them are factored in. This represents a 36% decline in rural population on the Aksumite Plateau since the Late Aksumite Period (comparing populations of the two periods outside the perimeters of their respective urban zones). This is less than half the decline noted for urban Aksum (77% vs 36%).

Despite this decline, and despite the disappearance of the *Adua Basin Chiefdom* site group, the distribution of rural sites and their association with *elite residential structures* argues strongly for the continued presence of a rural political infrastructure distinct from that of urban Aksum (See Figure 13).

THE EASTERN PERIPHERY CHIEFDOM

The *Eastern Periphery Chiefdom* (Figure 13) appears to carry over from the Late Aksumite Period without appreciable modification. It continues to occupy the eastern periphery of the Aksumite Plain, with its *hamlets* and *small villages* distributed along a north/south axis. The *elite residence* continues to be located at Enda Jesus. One principal difference, however, is the absence of any noticeable factory-scale workshop utilization of jasper tools.

THE SOUTHERN PERIPHERY CHIEFDOM

The *Southern Periphery Chiefdom* (Figure 13) also appears to represent continuity with the previous period despite the evident reduction in the number of settlements associated with it. However, unlike the Late Aksumite Period where no elite residence could be documented, a *palace-scale* elite residence is associated with the chiefdom during this period.

THE WESTERN PERIPHERY CHIEFDOM

The elite residence of the *Western Periphery Chiefdom* (Figure 13) continues to be of *palace-scale*, and it continues to be located on high ground overlooking the Fil Filli Valley, but the rural settlements believed to be associated with it are scattered around the far side of the *amba* to the southeast, in an area associated with the *Periphery Chiefdom* of the Late Aksumite Period. The ceramic attribute data, however, does not provide any corroborating evidence that would support the decision to group these sites into a distinct political unit. Nevertheless, the alternative hypothesis, namely that these *hamlets* are outlier settlements linked organizationally to urban Aksum, is called into doubt by the absence of the distinctive ceramic micro-tradition associated with urban Aksum in the ceramic assemblages of the *hamlets* in question.

THE NORTHERN PERIPHERY CHIEFDOM

The *Northern Periphery Chiefdom* is a collection of *hamlets* and *small villages* located in what used to be the northeastern quadrant of Metropolitan Aksum during the Late Aksumite Period. The presence of a rural political entity in that area is evidenced by the presence of a *palace-scale* elite residential complex at Adi Watot. As in the case of the *Western Periphery Chiefdom*, the hypothesis that these rural settlements are affiliated with urban Aksum is called into doubt by the absence of that center's distinctive ceramic micro-tradition among the ceramic assemblages of those sites. By default then, the rural settlements that lay between urban Aksum and the *palace* of Adi Watot—3 *hamlets* and 4 *small villages*—have been grouped together into a single rural political entity called the *Northern Periphery Chiefdom*.

THE POLITICAL IMPLICATIONS OF THE CERAMIC MICRO-TRADITION OF AKSUM

A comparison of the ceramic attribute data reveals a dramatic contrast between the ceramic profiles of the rural settlements on the Aksumite Plateau and urban Aksum respectively. To begin with, there is a significant difference with respect to the percentage of body sherds that exhibit decorative treatment: among the sites that form urban Aksum an average of 5.6% of body sherds show decorative treatment, whereas among site assemblages that represent rural settlement the average is 1%. Secondly, two of the most numerous attributes at urban Aksum—DT-*ribbed* and DT-*punctate*—are among the least numerous within assemblages of rural settlements. And finally, none of the assemblages among rural settlements are comparable to those of urban Aksum in exhibiting the full extent of the ceramic attribute complex, or *micro-tradition*, that distinguishes urban Aksum in the Early Post-Aksumite Period.

If the existence of a ceramic micro-tradition is evidence of what archaeologists refer to as an *interaction sphere*—a cluster of communities that exhibit inter-generational tendencies to largely confine social and economic intercourse to those persons contained within its boundaries—then one might argue that those communities that fall outside this *interaction sphere* constitute a separate socio-economic domain. And given the existence of multiple political nodes, as represented by *elite residential complexes*, one is compelled to question the assumption that urban Aksum enjoys political hegemony over the entire subregion of the Aksumite Plateau during the Early Post-Aksumite Period. This is particularly true when one considers that the *elite residential complexes* to be found among rural settlements are at parity in scale to the Jana Duk elite complex of urban Aksum, or even perhaps of greater scale.

What we seem to have, therefore, is a political environment on the Aksumite Plateau during the Early Post-Aksumite Period that consists of a tightly integrated urban settlement—Aksum—with its own leadership, and four local chiefdoms with which rural communities are associated and that enjoy political autonomy.

The fact that urban Aksum possessed a distinguished legacy of having once been the capital of the Aksumite Kingdom and, according to one of the inscriptions of Hadani Dan'el (Kobishchanov 1979:120), had a political ruler who bore the title of [vassal] *king*, does not—in this author's opinion—call into question the political scenario described above.

CHAPTER SEVEN
The Late Post-Aksumite Period

INTRODUCTION

Kobischanov, in his discussion of the political history of Aksum (Kobischanov 1979:121), raises the question as to which elements of the Aksumite population might have been involved in bringing Northern Ethiopian Christian culture to Central Ethiopia after the collapse of the Aksumite Kingdom. He assumes that monks and priests, as well as merchants, must have been involved, but wonders whether resettlement might also have involved those he refers to as peasants, and perhaps also members of the ruling elite. As we examine the archaeological record for the Late Post-Aksumite Period, the answer to Kobishchanov's question becomes readily apparent. We observe that not only have all vestiges of a secular elite disappeared from the Aksum-Yeha Survey Region, but that also there has been a profound evacuation of the region by both urban and rural non-elite populations (see Figure 14). One can reasonably conclude that the acculturative process by which northern Ethiopian Christian culture was introduced into central Ethiopia involved resettlement of regional populations such as the one now absent from our survey region. This remarkable shift in settlement from northern Ethiopia to central Ethiopia appears to have involved all facets of Aksumite society.

SETTLEMENT PATTERN SUMMARY

Urban Aksum has ceased to exist. The population of Urban Aksum in the Early Post-Aksumite Period was estimated at a little over 9,000 people. By the Late Post-Aksumite Period that community had disappeared. The only archaeological evidence of a residential presence at Aksum—detected so far—is that of what appears to have been a religious order at Enda Maryam, adjacent to the ancient church of Maryam Tseyon.

Rural population has declined from an estimated 1900 people in the Early Post-Aksumite Period to around 600 people in the Late Post-Aksumite Period—a 69% reduction that involved the elimination of the settlements of the *Eastern Periphery Chiefdom* and of the *Northern Periphery Chiefdom*.

The population that chose to remain in the survey region did so with some trepidation—one must assume—since without exception their *hamlets* and *villages* were concealed among boulders high up on the slopes of mountains and *ambas*, or otherwise positioned in inconspicuous settings that would not attract the attention of those passing through the region on the well-established routes. This suggests that the region either did not enjoy the protection of a political entity that could defend its frontiers, or that the rulers of the protective realm were themselves an exploitative element to be avoided.

An apparent consequence of this defensive settlement pattern was likely to have been the inability of the region's farmers to fully exploit the most favorable soils—those of the Plain of Aksum—for the cultivation of fields out on the open plain would have drawn the attention of those passing through, and would thereby have compromised the effort at concealment reflected in the settlement pattern. This represents an historic reversal of a trend towards greater and greater utilization of the Plain of Aksum, and other more favorable soils, that began in the Late Pre-Aksumite Period after the collapse of the Yeha Polity with its penchant for irrigation agriculture. The inadvisability of exploiting the most favorable soils may have also contributed in some measure to the scale of population reduction in the area.

DiBlasi (2004c) also suggests that drought conditions may have become more frequent and severe during the Post-Aksumite Era, and that this might have served as an additional inducement for communities to relocate to the central highlands where rainfall regimes were more favorable.

All settlements, with one exception, fall within the *hamlet* or *small village* categories, with an average estimated residential population of less than two dozen people. Such small communities would have been more successful at concealing their presence, and would have been more capable of sustaining themselves utilizing less optimal ecozones.

The one exception, however, is of considerable interest. It is the *large village* of Guadguad Agazien, located at the far northern edge of the summit of *Amba Bieta Giyorgis*. This community, estimated to have accommodated over 400 people, represents 68% of the total estimated population of the region, and thus could be reasonably considered the core resident population of the Aksumite Plateau during the Late Post-Aksumite Period.

The fact that such a large number of people chose to reside together in a single community suggests a level of social affinity that most likely rests upon deep inter-generational ties. And the fact that they could sustain such a large co-residency demonstrates the strategic isolation of the far northern portion of the *amba* summit. But of greatest interest is the possibility that the residents of Guadguad Agazien represent the descendants of the Late Pre-Aksumite polity of Bieta Giyorgis that are believed to have originally initiated the rise of the Aksumite Kingdom through trade with kingdoms along the Nile River, and who eventually shifted their residence to Aksum proper as their political organization evolved from that of a subregional chiefdom to that of an interregional kingdom. Under this scenario, some fraction of the core population of Aksumites sought out the protection of their ancestral lands on the top of *Amba Bieta Giyorgis* in the face of an ever more hostile political environment.

Joseph W. Michels

THE CHRISTIAN CHURCH AS AN INSTRUMENT OF POLITICAL INTEGRATION

When we examine regional political organization of the Aksumite Plateau during the Late Post-Aksumite Period, in the face of the abandonment of the area by the secular elite, as well as by most of the urban and rural population, we observe the ascendancy of the Christian Church as an instrument of political integration. Our best example is that of the *Western Periphery* local chiefdom of the Early Post-Aksumite Period. An examination of Figure 14 reveals a hypothetical polity of the Late Post-Aksumite Period that was centered on the church of Enda Michael. The reader will observe that this church was built upon the ruins of the *palace* of Enda Michael, which is believed to have been the residence of the secular elite who governed that chiefdom during the preceding period. And the spatial cluster of communities believed to have constituted the polity remained remarkably similar as the Early Post-Aksumite Period gave way to the Late Post-Aksumite Period.

If we assume such a model applies, then the archaeological remains of the small churches of Enda Michael, Adi Takana, and Enda Cerqos offer some evidence for the presence of three church-centered polities on the Aksumite Plateau (see Figure 14). The absence of affiliated settlements with the Enda Cerqos polity, and the presence of only a single settlement in the Adi Takana polity, would suggest either that the settlements are located in areas not sampled during our survey, or that these two polities came into existence sufficiently late in the sequence that antecedent communities underlying contemporary settlements were the constituent members. The architectural style of the two churches in question might very well support the latter interpretation (see Contenson 1961b).

The existence of a fourth polity, located at Aksum, would seem to be entirely likely given the presence of the religious community at Enda Maryam, located adjacent to the ancient church of Maryam Tseyon. In fact, the absence of any residential annex among the ruins of the churches of Adi Takana and Enda Cerqos raises the possibility that Enda Maryam served as the principal residence of the outlying clergy, who occupied ordinary dwellings within one of the settlements of their respective polity during their stay. Other members of the religious order at Enda Maryam would have been available to attend to those activities associated with the presence of the church of Maryam Tseyon, as well as to the pastoral needs of the Aksum polity. The exercise of secular influence by the Ethiopian Christian Church, a practice believed to have commenced during the Late Aksumite Period (see Chapter 5), would seem to have persisted right up to the ethnographic present (see e.g. Simoons 1960:27-28).

BIBLIOGRAPHIC RESOURCES USED IN THE PREPARATION OF THE UNABRIDGED PUBLICATION

Anfray, Francis, 1963. Une Campagne de Fouilles B Yeha. *Annales D'Ethiopie* V: 171-232. Addis Ababa.

Anfray, Francis, 1965. Chronique Archeologique (1960-1964). *Annales D'Ethiopie VI*: 3-48. Addis Ababa.

Anfray, Francis, 1968. Aspects de L'Archéologie Éthiopienne. *Journal of African History* (Vol. IX, No. 3, pp. 345-366. London.

Anfray, Francis, 1972a. Fouilles de Yeha. *Annales D'Ethiopie* IX: 45-64. Addis Ababa.

Anfray, Francis. 1972b. L'Archéologie D'Axoum en 1972. *Paideuma XVIII*: 60-78.

Anfray, Francis, 1973a. Nouveaux Sites Antiques. *Journal of Ethiopian Studies* XI (No. 2): 13-27. Addis Ababa.

Anfray, Francis, 1973b. Les Fouilles de Yeha. *Documents Pour Servir a L'Histoire des Civilizations Ethiopiennes* IV: 35-38. Centre National de la Recherche Scientifique, Paris.

Anfray, Francis, 1974. Deux Villes Axoumites: Adoulis et Matara. *Proceedings of the IV Congresso Internazionale di Studi Etiopici* (Vol. 1): 745-772. Roma, Accademia Nazionale Dei Lincei.

Ascher, Marcia and Robert Ascher, 1963. Chronological Ordering by Computer. *American Anthropologist* 65 (No. 5): 1045-1052.

Bard, Kathryn and Michael C. DiBlasi, Rodolfo Fattovich, Andrea Manzo, Cinzia Perlingieri, A. Catherine D'Andrea, Louis Chaix, Raymond A. Silverman, Neal W. Sobania, Erica Puntel. 1998. The IUO and BU Archaeological Expedition at Bieta Giyorgis (Aksum): 1998 Field Season. *Technical Report to the Center for Research and Conservation of the Cultural Heritage, Ministry of Information and Culture, Addis Ababa, Ethiopia.* Boston-Naples: Boston University.

Bauer, Dan Franz. 1977. *Household and Society in Ethiopia: An Economic and Social Analysis of Tigray Social Principles and Household Organization.* Monograph No. 6, Occasional Papers Series, Northeast African Studies Committee. East Lansing, Michigan State University.

Blalock, Hubert M. 1960. *Social Statistics.* New York: McGraw Hill.

Brainerd, George W. 1951. The Place of Chronological Ordering in Archaeological Analysis. *American Antiquity* 16 (No. 4): 303-313.

Butzer, Karl W. 1981. Rise and Fall of Axum, Ethiopia: A Geo-Archaeological Interpretation. *American Antiquity* 46: 471-495.

Chittick, H. Neville. 1974. Excavations at Aksum, 1973-74: A Preliminary Report. *Azania* IX:159-205.

Connah, Graham. 1987. *African Civilizations: Precolonial Cities and States in Tropical Africa, an Archaeological Perspective.* Cambridge: Cambridge University Press.

Contenson, Henri de. 1959. Les Fouilles à Axoum en 1957: Rapport Preliminaire. *Annales D'Ethiopie* 3:25-42.

Contenson, Henri de. 1961a. Trouvailles Fortuites Aux Environs D'Axoum. *Annales D'Ethiopie* 4: 15-38.

Contenson, Henri de. 1961b. Les Fouilles à Haoulti-Melazo in 1958. *Annales D'Ethiopie* 4: 39-60.

Contenson, Henri de. 1961c. Les Fouilles à Ouchatei Golo, Près D'Axoum, en 1958. *Annales D'Ethiopie* 4:1-14.

Contenson, Henri de. 1963a. Les Fouilles à Axoum en 1958: Rapport Preliminaire. *Annales D'Ethiopie* 5:1-40.

Contenson, Henri de. 1963b. Les Fouilles à Haoulti en 1959: Rapport Preliminaire. *Annales D'Ethiopie* 5:41-86,

Craytor, William Bert and LeRoy Johnson, Jr. 1968. *Refinements in Computerized Item Seriation, Bulletin No. 10.* Eugene: Museum of Natural History, University of Oregon.

DiBlasi, Michael C. 2003a. *Personal Communication.* Email dtd. 11/12/2003

DiBlasi, Michael C. 2003b. *Personal Communication.* Email dtd. 12/11/2003

DiBlasi, Michael C. 2004a. *Personal Communication.* Email dtd. 6/16/2004.

DiBlasi, Michael C. 2004b. *Personal Communication.* Email dtd. 5/2004.

DiBlasi, Michael C. 2004c. *Personal Communication.* Email dtd. 6/2004.

Drewes, A.J., 1959. Les Inscriptions de Melazo. *Annales D'Ethiopie* III: 83-99. Addis Abba.

Fattovich, Rodolfo, 1998. *The Archaeological Expedition in Ethiopia (Aksum) of the Istituto Universitario Orientale and Boston University.* Addis Ababa: The Italian Cultural Institute.

Fattovich, Rodolfo; Kathryn A. Bard; Lorenzo Petrassi; and Vincenzo Pisano. 2000. *The Aksum Archaeological Area: A Preliminary Assessment.* Naples: Istituto Universitario Orientale.

Gibbon, Edward. 1952. *The Decline and Fall of the Roman Empire,* 2 vols. Chicago: Encyclopaedia Britannica, Inc.

Johnson, Jr., LeRoy. 1968. *Item Seriation as an Aid for Elementary Scale and Cluster Analysis, Bulletin No. 15.* Eugene: Museum of Natural History, University of Oregon.

Kasmin, V. 1973. *Geological Map of Ethiopia.* Addis Ababa: Ethiopian Ministry of Mines

Kobishchanov, Yuri M. 1979. *Axum,* trans. L.T. Kapitanoff, ed. J.W. Michels. University Park and London: The Pennsylvania State University Press.

Krencker, Daniel 1913. Ältere Denkmäler Nordabessiniens. *Deutsche Aksum-Expedition, Vol. II.* Berlin: George Reimer, Publisher.

Lebedev, A.N., editor. 1970. *The Climate of Africa, Part 1 – Air Temperature, Precipitation.* Translated from Russian. Jerusalem: Israel Program for Scientific Translations

Leclant, Jean. 1959a. Les Fouilles a Axoum en 1955-1956: Rapport Preliminare. *Annales D'Ethiopie* III: 3-24.

Leclant, Jean. 1959b. Haoulti-Melazo (1955-1956). *Annales d'Ethiopie*, III:43-82, Addis Ababa.

Lee, Richard. 1969. Chemical Temperature Integration. *Journal of Applied Meteorology* 8(3): 423.

Littman, Enno. 1913. Reisebericht Der Expedition Topograhie Und Geschichte Aksums. *Deutsche Aksum-Expedition, Vol. I.* Berlin: George Reimer, Publisher.

Lüpke, Von Th. V. 1913. Reste Eines Tempels des Ares auf Abba Pantaleon bei Aksum. In Ältere Denkmäler Nordabessiniens, *Deutsche Aksum-Expedition, Vol. II: 90-94* by Daniel Krencker. Berlin: George Reimer, Publisher.

Michels, Joseph W. 1979. Axumite Archaeology: An Introductory Essay. In *Axum*, by Yuri M. Kobishchanov, trans. L.T. Kapitanoff, ed. J.W. Michels, 1-34. University Park and London: The Pennsylvania State University Press.

Michels, Joseph W. 1982 Bulk Element Composition Versus Trace Element Composition in the Reconstruction of an Obsidian Source System. *Journal of Archaeological Science* 9: 113-123.

Michels, Joseph W. 1994. Regional Political Organization in the Axum-Yeha Area During the Preaxumite and Axumite Eras. *Études Éthiopiennes* I: 61-80.

Michels, Joseph W., Ignatius S.T. Tsong and Charles M. Nelson. 1983. Obsidian Dating and East African Archeology. *Science* 219: 361-366.

Munro-Hay, Stuart C. 1989. *Excavations at Aksum*. London: The British Institute in Eastern Africa.

Munro-Hay, Stuart C. 1991. *Aksum: An African Civilization of Late Antiquity*. Edinburgh: Edinburgh University Press.

Philipson, David W. 1995. Excavations at Aksum, Ethiopia, 1993-4. *The Antiquaries Journal 75:1-41*.

Phillipson, David W. 1998. *Ancient Ethiopia: Aksum, Its Antecedents and Successors*. London: British Museum Press.

Phillipson, David W. 2000. *Archaeology at Aksum, Ethiopia, 1993-7* (2 Vols.). London: The British Institute in Eastern Africa.

Pirenne, Jacqueline. 1970. Haoulti, Gobochela (Melazo) et le site antique. *Annales d'Ethiopie,* VIII: 117-127, Addis Ababa.

Puglisi, Salvatore. 1941. Primi risultati delle indagini compiute dalla Missione Archeologica di Aksum. *Africa Italiana, VIII*: 95-153.

Ricci, Lanfranco. 1974. Scavi archeologici in Etiopia. *Africa,* XXIX (3): 435-441, Rome.

Schoff, S. Wilfred (tr. & ed.), 1912. *The Periplus of the Erythraean Sea: Travel and Trade in the Indian Ocean by a Merchant of the First Century. London, Bombay & Calcutta.*

Simoons, Frederick J. 1960. *Northwest Ethiopia: Peoples and Economy*. Madison: The University of Wisconsin Press.

Van Beek, G. W. 1969. The Rise and Fall of Arabia Felix. *Scientific American* 221: 36-46.

Wernstedt, Frederick L. 1972. *World Climatic Data*. State College, PA: Climatic Data Press.

Winstedt, E.O. 1899. *The Christian Topography of Cosmas Indicopleustes*. Cambridge.

Printed by BoD"in Norderstedt, Germany